The King
Who Lost America

The King
Who Lost America

GEORGE III
AND INDEPENDENCE

by

Allen Andrews

JUPITER BOOKS LIMITED
167 Hermitage Road
London N4

TO THE CROWN JEWEL

First published in 1976 by
Jupiter Books (London) Limited
167 Hermitage Road, London N4

SBN 904041 549

Copyright © Allen Andrews 1976

Set in 12/14pt. Monotype Garamond 156
and printed and bound by
R. J. Acford Limited, Chichester

Contents

The King Who Lost America
page 11

Appendices

Select Bibliography

The King
Who Lost America

By the KING,

A PROCLAMATION,

For fuppreffing Rebellion and Sedition.

GEORGE R.

 HEREAS many of Our Subjects in divers Parts of Our Colonies and Plantations in *North America*, misled by dangerous and ill-designing Men, and forgetting the Allegiance which they owe to the Power that has protected and suftained them, after various diforderly Acts committed in Difturbance of the Publick Peace, to the Obftruction of lawful Commerce, and to the Oppreffion of Our loyal Subjects carrying on the fame, have at length proceeded to an open and avowed Rebellion, by arraying themfelves in hoftile Manner to withftand the Execution of the Law, and traitoroufly preparing, ordering, and levying War against Us· And whereas there is Reafon to apprehend that fuch Rebellion hath been much promoted and encouraged by the traitorous Correfpondence, Counfels, and Comfort of divers wicked and defperate Perfons within this Realm : To the End therefore that none of Our Subjects may neglect or violate their Duty through Ignorance thereof, or through any Doubt of the Protection which the Law will afford to their Loyalty and Zeal ; We have thought fit, by and with the Advice of Our Privy Council, to iffue this Our Royal Proclamation, hereby declaring that not only all Our Officers Civil and Military are obliged to exert their utmoft Endeavours to fupprefs fuch Rebellion, and to bring the Traitors to Juftice ; but that all Our Subjects of this Realm and the Dominions thereunto belonging are bound by Law to be aiding and affifting in the Suppreffion of fuch Rebellion, and to difclofe and make known all traitorous Confpiracies and Attempts against Us, Our Crown and Dignity ; And We do accordingly ftrictly charge and command all Our Officers as well Civil as Military, and all other Our obedient and loyal Subjects, to ufe their utmoft Endeavours to withftand and fupprefs fuch Rebellion, and to difclofe and make known all Treafons and traitorous Confpiracies which they fhall know to be against Us, Our Crown and Dignity ; and for that Purpofe, that they tranfmit to One of Our Principal Secretaries of State, or other proper Officer, due and full Information of all Perfons who fhall be found carrying on Correfpondence with, or in any Manner or Degree aiding or abetting the Perfons now in open Arms and Rebellion against Our Government within any of Our Colonies and Plantations in *North America*, in order to bring to condign Punifhment the Authors, Perpetrators, and Abettors of fuch traitorous Defigns.

Given at Our Court at St. *James's*, the Twenty-third Day of *Auguft*, One thousand feven hundred and feventy-five, in the Fifteenth Year of Our Reign.

God fave the King.

LONDON:

Printed by *Charles Eyre* and *William Strahan*, Printers to the King's moft Excellent Majefty. 1775.

Gainsborough pinxt about the Year 1765.　　Hopwood Sculpt.

HIS MOST GRACIOUS MAJESTY KING GEORGE THE THIRD.
Born May 24 O.S. 1738.

CHARLES, PRINCE OF WALES, WROTE RECENTLY THAT HIS ancestor, King George III, had borne for far too long 'the stigma of madness'. The Prince of Wales said that his great-great-great-great-great grandfather was not schizophrenic, nor depressive, and did not suffer from syphilis of the central nervous system – the condition which leads to GPI, general paralysis of the insane. Rather, said Prince Charles, his predecessor as Prince of Wales 225 years ago suffered from attacks of a physical disease. 'There was nothing wrong with his brain *before* the onset of the illness,' declared the present Heir to the Throne, although he conceded that after 1788 King George III did display some 'rather dotty behaviour'.

The date 1788 is five years after the peace which recognised the independence of the United States of America, and twelve years after the coining of that phrase in the Declaration of Independence which blasted him as 'unfit to be the ruler of a free people'. Prince Charles has absolved his ancestor from any charge that 'the King who lost America' was dotty at the time.

The Prince of Wales has, of course, a vested interest in establishing that his forebear did not deserve 'the stigma of madness', although it is, perhaps, less of a stigma than he thinks. The alternative explanations of the behaviour of the King at odd times during his fifties and sixties, and for the last years of his very long life are (1) an undefined metabolic illness, which the

13

*Stripped of wig and breeches, the inmates
of Bedlam were portrayed by Hogarth
for* The Rake's Progress.
MARY EVANS COLLECTION

Prince fancies; (2) porphyria, a hereditary disease named after one of its symptoms, the passing of purple urine; (3) senility.

Senility is a condition common to all who can hang on to life until they reach it; nobody can be proud of it, but it is no great stigma. Porphyria has been traced in the family of King George III, back as far as Mary Queen of Scots and forward to touch descendants of that Queen now living. There have been other hereditary diseases in the British Royal Family, including haemophilia, the bleeding disease. They are nothing to boast about, but also nothing to defend with any great vehemence – mere misfortunes which must be accepted. But surely the same is true of madness. We have all had mad ancestors and many of us will have mad descendants, and we should not be over-sensitive about any supposed 'stigma'.

My own great-great-great-great-great grandfather, Dr Robert Andrews of Bloomsbury (and later of Bedlam), was undoubtedly mad according to the standards of his time, and after two centuries I really cannot bestir myself to prove that he should be given a more respectable label, and carry a new ticket on the crumbling bones of his big toe naming some recently discovered disease. In any case, he provided acceptable entertainment as a lunatic on show at Bedlam (a stout building the successor to which now houses the Imperial War Museum). And even though – or, perhaps, because – he was bonkers, he displayed a pretty wit. King George III had the same illuminating wisdom. When he protested at the hard treatment administered to him by one of his doctors, who did little more than strap him up in a strait-waistcoat and pour buckets of cold water over his Sovereign, the doctor – a religious man, but a smug one – gave the unctuous reminder: 'Sir, our Saviour himself went about healing the sick.' 'Yes, yes,' the King countered, 'but he had not £700 a year for it.' In fact the annual fees paid to the King's 'mad doctors' averaged £35,000 a year in good eighteenth-century money.

My own great-great-great-great-great grandfather was philosophical even about the indignity of being exhibited naked to curious spectators who went to Bedlam to see the savage lunatics as the equivalent of a modern trip to the zoo. To a friend who sympathised with him over the 'inhumanity' of such display he observed, 'Sir, stripped of my wig and breeches, I am no less human than I was. I trust that the gawping public will see themselves more clearly when they gaze on me.'

This perceptive voice from the age of George III can throw an invaluable light on the personality and actions of King George himself. Today we are unnecessarily confused by the physical image we retain of the King who lost America. He is a theatrical figure in a wig and knee-breeches, an Emperor wearing too many clothes, distorted for us by the uniform and speech of his period into an unreal talking waxwork with whom we cannot

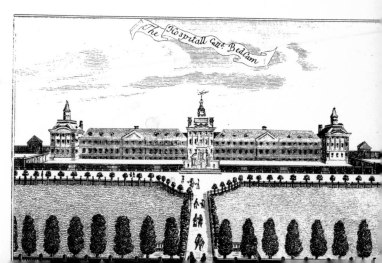

Bethlehem Hospital, alias Bedlam, before it fell down and Liverpool Street Station was built on the site.
MARY EVANS COLLECTION

relate. Strip King George of his wig and breeches, and we may find a recognisable and even a sympathetic character.

THE JUVENILE TYCOON

In modern plutocratic terms George was the fourth-generation sprig of a family of corporation millionaires. He knew that, owing to the death of his father, he would be called to take over the business before he could acquire adequate experience. On the one hand he was highly apprehensive about his inadequacy at man-management. On the other hand, he held strong theories about how to run the business, and these clashed at almost every point with the policy of his grandfather, still in the chair. He was in a fever to take over control, yet nervous in the realisation that he would need to fire most of the standing board of directors before his control would be positive.

His only support was the knowledge that he had one older man waiting in the wings to bolster his courage as soon as he took over, and to this man he gave not only extravagant political reliance but also a highly emotional affection.

But George's link with this man alienated him from the men who were running the corporation before his take-over of power, and particularly from his grandfather, who still sat at the head of the board, and would continue to do so until he died and George succeeded him.

The antipathy arose because the man who was George's demi-god was not only unpopular for his person and his policies, but was reputed to be the lover of George's mother, George's father being dead.

And this scandal, which was well known as a rumour to the emotionally immature George – though he did not believe it – had a further complicated influence on his development and on the future of the corporation he was to manage. Firstly it shocked him to the core, for he was an extremely pious man and remained so throughout his life. Secondly, he over-reacted to the prevalent gossip centring on the scandal. Instead of accepting muck-spreading as part of the rough-and-tumble of big business, he took the matter too seriously.

THE PRICE OF HIS MOTHER'S HONOUR

He swore a mighty oath to his adored adviser, who was enduring the after-effects of the scandal along with his mother:

GEORGE the THIRD,

In the 1st Year of his Reign.

London, Published by Thos Kelly, 17, Paternoster Row, Feb.7.1820.

'*I am young and inexperienced and want advice.*'

MARY EVANS COLLECTION

I do therefore here in the presence of Our Almighty Lord promise that I will ever remember the insults done to my mother, and never will forgive anyone who shall offer to speak disrespectfully of her.

This teenage oath, and the intensity with which it was kept in one particular instance, was the stream of fire which burnt out all George's reasonableness, extinguished his capacity to compromise, and by a peculiar combination of circumstances groomed him for the tossing away of America. It is obvious over-simplification to say that England lost America because of George III's concern for his mother's honour. England and America were destined to part because of built-in English and American attitudes which were mutually derived from English concepts of liberty and responsibility but which sparked against each other rather than fused into union – mainly because of eighteenth-century non-communication and non-adaptation of the current. It is no exaggeration to say, however, that George III personally, though unwillingly, threw away America because of his irrational pursuit of the oath he took about his mother's virtue, and the unforeseeable consequences of that action on his unsophisticated character. George III had a narrow mind, but a deep one. If his brow could accommodate only a few furrows, they held acid which etched into his brain almost with the impact of leucotomy.

GREAT BRITAIN INC.

What was the corporation to which George III stood as immature heir? It was, officially, the United Kingdom of Great Britain, France* and Ireland, together with the very vast spaces of the British Empire which had recently been acquired, and the essential Dukedom of Brunswick and Luneburg, a tiny jewel in the Crown, but the only reason why the family of The Georges was wearing the diadem. This last territory was always popularly known as the Electorate of Hanover, because of its relationship to the Holy Roman Empire, and the only claim which George III advanced as heir to the corporation was the piece of scrip affirming that his ancestors had held this small German state.

The Hanoverian Succession in England was a last-ditch attempt by the English Parliament to ensure that the British Monarchy was WASP. Since the White Anglo-Saxon requirements could then be taken for granted, the

---

* Kings of England had styled themselves Kings of France since the Hundred Years War. George III dropped the title in 1801.

only practical necessity was to ensure that those who ascended the throne were of the Protestant faith. The Act of Succession was debated and passed by Parliament in 1701, just as coolly and legalistically as the debating and enactment of the Abortion Bill in the 1960s. The laws of Britain were carefully and precisely changed to state that on the death of Queen Anne, who was the last Protestant monarch of the Stuart Royal Family, the throne should pass to the Protestant issue of the only remote, female, descendant of the Stuarts who remained Protestant. She was Sophia, a niece of King Charles I who had married Duke Ernest Augustus of Hanover in 1658. The Electress Sophia lived for 56 years after her marriage. She was Heir Presumptive during the thirteen years of the reign of Queen Anne, and Heir Apparent after 1708, on the death of Anne's husband, Prince George of Denmark, at a time when the Queen was past child-bearing capacity – the couple had fourteen children, but only one survived infancy, and he was dead by 1700.

Sophia died, aged 84, a few weeks before Queen Anne. Her son, therefore, a German princeling, then in his fifty-fourth year, came to England, mounted the throne with great satisfaction, brought in troops to quell a rebellion in favour of the ousted male Stuarts, and stole back to enjoy the more sensual delights of Hanover whenever he could persuade Parliament

AUGUSTA Princess Dowager of WALES.

Falsely reputed to have Bute in her bed, but correctly reported to have him in her bedroom: Augusta, Dowager Princess of Wales, mother of George III.
MARY EVANS COLLECTION

Press-ganged for the Navy – 'no great menace to the liberties of the landed gentry.'
MARY EVANS COLLECTION

that he needed to take time off. After 14 years he died and made room for his son, 44 years old, who was to reign until he was 77.

HANOVERIAN RELUCTANCE

These first German Kings were George I and George II in the century-old business known as The Four Georges. Historians used to teach that George I could speak no English and George II was interested only in women, wine and war, in that order, and consequently they left the business of governing Britain to professional politicians, and so established the country as a pioneer of parliamentary democracy. Almost every word of this analysis is wrong. George I could speak little English – yet at least enough for him to say: 'I hate all Boets and Bainters,' which gets him consistently into quotation dictionaries. But George I's ministers did most of their business with him, not in dog-Latin, as Walpole's son embroidered, but in French, which everyone in educated circles could then use in a version that was less comic than Winston Churchill's or Ted Heath's. George II and his Queen spoke French consistently to each other, which led to George II's solitary entry in the quotation books:

Caroline, dying, urged George to take another wife.
GEORGE II: *Non, j'aurai des maîtresses* [No, I shall take mistresses].
CAROLINE: *Ah! Mon Dieu! Cela n'empêche pas* [Oh, God, that's no problem].

Language had little influence on the political impact of the first two Georges. They were uninterested in the details of domestic government as long as they could keep foreign policy as firmly as possible in their hands – which they mainly did – and particularly the issues of peace and war. All they wanted from their British subjects was the money to pursue foreign policy, raised by taxes passed in Parliament. They did not even seek British bodies for their armies, because they could buy better troops abroad. But they did relish the use of the Royal Navy – they had never owned even a Royal Bumboat before. And Parliament, though always afraid of the menace of a standing army, did oblige by allowing Britons to be press-ganged into the Navy, since they considered that jolly Jack Tars, carefully confined when off duty to hulks in the Medway and Solent with only occasional raids on the town brothels, were no great menace to the liberties of the landed gentry.

EUREKA! A PRIME MINISTER!

The first two Georges wanted *managers* who would assure the limited independence sought by the monarchs. They hit on the happy invention of a Prime Minister, who could do most of the dirty work, politically speaking, on their behalf. They gave their confidence to a politician who could demonstrate that he had the confidence and support of Parliament – always provided that the chosen man was loyal to the continuance of the Hanoverian succession. It was a fairly fool-proof policy. The Prime Minister had to be competent in order to manage the House of Commons, and compliant in order to please the King. Once these qualities were assured – or seemed to be assured, for a really competent man like Sir Robert Walpole could fool the King with compliance and yet often get his own way through pleading unavoidable pressures – the King passed over enough power to keep the politician massively interested in staying.

WILLIAM PITT, EARL OF CHATHAM.

OB. 1778.

FROM THE ORIGINAL OF HOARE, IN THE COLLECTION OF

THE RIGHT HON^{ble} LORD BRIDPORT.

The hand-out which the King bestowed was the provision of almost un-limited access to power and riches. Politics was not pure. It was the quick route to a large fortune because of the enormous perquisites of office – a fact which has never been ignored in America, but was forgotten in Great Britain for a century after Victoria's succession and is only now beginning to be re-appreciated. Prime Ministers could not only make a packet for themselves, but could promise the prospect of speedy riches for those who supported them. Those in the political game who were little concerned with additional wealth, men like the large land-owners with estates almost ranging over entire counties, could still be tempted with the reward of titles.

The King, as the fount of honour, re-channelled the honours racket to his Prime Minister, who had the self-satisfaction of being courted on ac-count of his power as well as the comfort of lining his pockets with the pensions and percentage commissions drawn from his own sinecure offices and his control over raising government loans. Lord Mayors could be made baronets, country gentlemen could be created barons, earls could be advanced to marquisates. If anybody ever paused to work out the intricate worthlessness of nobility bought by bribery, he would be pulled up sharp by a realisation of the massively extended credit which a title ensured – or by the snobbish protestations of his wife. Today, half the men who chase a title excuse themselves by saying that they are doing it only for the sake of the little woman. In the eighteenth century even the elder William Pitt, before he consented to assume the Earldom of Chatham, had stretched his pride sufficiently to request a separate peerage for his wife on account of services rendered – rendered by Pitt, one should hasten to add, and not by Lady Hester. But the case of Pitt confirms that even in his age there was a strong popular backlash about the virtual corruption involved in the bestowal of titles. Pitt had been known in the country as The Great Commoner. When he took the Chatham title he was engulfed by a most unexpected wave of democratic disapproval – and his style was instantly converted to 'Lord Cheat'em'.

The Prime Minister, through the power he held to bestow wealth and titles among the comparatively small governing class of Great Britain, managed Parliament and, as the King's political pimp, provided the monarch with his ambitious pleasures in the sphere of world politics. There were two snags to the system. The first was that almost half of the country was disenfranchised – even if the then governing class alone is considered – for the Tory party was never recognised as corporately suitable for office over 75 years, until it had painfully proved that it had lost its taint of possible adherence to the Stuart dynasty, or at least to Stuart principles of autocratic government.

The second snag was that the system encouraged an unparliamentary opposition to the King's régime, wielding power in the House of Commons but not ultimately based in the House of Commons. Rather, it stemmed from the personality and power of the King's heir.

FILIAL FRICTION

Royal fathers have always quarrelled with royal sons, but no kings ever cursed their heirs as fervently as the Royal Georges (and even Victoria) damned their Princes of Wales. In every European country the Heir to the Throne was a nonentity until the day his father died – except in Great Britain. In Britain the King's eldest son was automatically Duke of Cornwall, and was therefore in the eighteenth century not only an extensive landowner but a potent political figure. For Devon and Cornwall, where the estates lay, held proportionately more rotten boroughs than any other territory. That is to say, they controlled the entry to an excessive number of seats in the House of Commons where the local elections could be decided by the votes of perhaps only a dozen resident voters – and their votes could be bought. The Prince of Wales thus became not only a highly influential figure because he was to be the next king, but his influence could be backed if necessary by votes in Parliament. Throughout the eighteenth century, for psychological as well as political reasons, the Princes of Wales were always on the worst of terms with their fathers – when the father of George III died as Frederick Prince of Wales, George Prince of Wales succeeded as inheritor of the antipathy towards George II – and this produced an artificially powerful cabal of opposition to the accepted policies of the ruling régime.

It also generated in the monarchs intense hatred for their eldest sons, but it must be said that when the turn of George III came the emotion was more of pain than of odium. George I exiled his own Prince of Wales, later George II, from his Court three years after he succeeded to the throne. But no Prince of Wales was more thoroughly detested by his parents than the son of George II, and father of George III, Frederick Lewis, Prince of Wales from his father's accession in 1727 until his perhaps

'Look, there he goes – that wretch – that villain! I wish the ground would open this moment to sink the monster to the lowest hole in hell.' Frederick ('Poor Fred') Prince of Wales, father of George III, became used to this sort of welcome from his hating mother, Queen Caroline.

MARY EVANS COLLECTION

timely death at the age of 44 in 1751. Poor Fred's mother, Queen Caroline, was the more vocal, 'Look, there he goes – that wretch! – that villain! – I wish the ground would open this moment and sink the monster to the lowest hole in hell!' Even on her deathbed the Queen found a consolation, 'At least I shall have one comfort in having my eyes eternally closed – I shall never see that monster again.'

THE SCOT IN THE BEDCHAMBER

Frederick tactfully waited fourteen years before confronting his mother in Hades. But he left a competent deputy to disturb the Royal Family. The year before he died, he introduced a 37 years old Scotsman into his household – John Stuart, Earl of Bute, whom he had picked up to make a set at a card table at Egham Races. Bute, a handsome but extremely pompous man, soon won his way into the affections of both Frederick and his wife Augusta, Princess of Wales. Frederick got him a sinecure post with a grand title – for which Bute had to do nothing except draw a fat pension – and appointed him Lord of the Bedchamber in his household. Society said

'Strutting Scotch peer', John Stuart,
Earl of Bute, 'court minion whose feeble
pretensions require the prostitution of
royalty for their support,' said Wilkes.
MARY EVANS COLLECTION

that this was the precise post which was unofficially granted to Bute by the
Princess of Wales. It is doubtful. The Princess and the Earl were assuredly
not lovers in Frederick's lifetime (though Fred had his own mistresses) and
there is no evidence beyond vague gossip that they became so afterwards.
Certainly there is no sociological evidence – they were both too refined to
use physical contraception – the sheep-gut condom might be used by
cruder Scots like Boswell, but only as a barrier against pox. They were

26

both highly fertile, Augusta was only 32, had borne nine children, and was not brought to bed again.

Certainly Bute came to her bedroom. There was a peculiar intimacy between them which granted him the exclusive right to the backstairs, and he used it to excess, staying many hours at a time with the Princess. But his familiarity should be credited rather to his ambition than his lust. He had cultivated Frederick as a ladder to political power. During his lifetime the Prince of Wales was highly influential and widely courted – his mother characteristically observing, 'My God, popularity always makes me sick, but Fritz's popularity makes me vomit.' On Fritz's death his twelve-year-old son George was speedily created Prince of Wales, but he had no right to the estates, income and political influence of the Duchy of Cornwall. This was reserved to the eldest son of the reigning King, but not to his heir

George III with his brother the Duke of York at the time of the death of their father.
NATIONAL PORTRAIT GALLERY

George III in childhood – he never had time to follow Hanoverian tradition and intrigue against his father.

MANSELL COLLECTION

before accession, and it was promptly grabbed back by George II, who decided he could use the £14,000 income and the control of the parliamentary boroughs to much better advantage himself.

GULLIBLE DEVOTION

The new Prince of Wales therefore had no major political influence based on parliamentary voting during the rest of the reign of George II. Consequently Bute could be excused if he considered that he had backed an eventual loser at the Egham Races. But his enemies underestimated his shrewdness. His target was the post of personal tutor to Augusta's son, George Prince of Wales, and in 1755 he achieved it. It was true that acceptance of him had to be forced through active opposition from the Cabinet and the irascible 72-year-old King George II. But the appointment was sanctioned.

Once Bute had secured this position, he assured himself that his future was made. He had only to keep on his existing intimate terms with Princess Augusta, and retain the unsuspicious confidence of Prince George of Wales, and he had first option on the post of Prime Minister as soon as his pupil ascended the throne as King George III.

He succeeded in these ambitions. He gained George's warm trust as an adviser, propagated from the very beginning his own political theories, and in addition inspired in the future George III an emotion which it is no exaggeration to describe as love. But no one had ever played for George's love before.

Bute's political philosophy – it was always philosophy, since it was never tempered by the pragmatism and need to compromise accepted by the really effective politician – was clearcut and of the most lasting influence on King George III. He taught the orthodox Whig view of the Constitution – in itself a surprisingly liberal, but not democratic, analysis which (if they would only bother to read it) would flummox those who out of sheer habit blindly allege that George III aimed to be a despotic monarch far more tyrannous than the Stuarts. The Whigs (who, after all, invented the new Constitution) believed that they had devised an intricate system of checks and balances between the people, their elected and nominated representatives, the officers of justice, the executive leadership and the sovereign power at the top of the pyramid – all subject to responsible public criticism – which it was almost impossible to improve. (The framers of the American Constitution thought the same.) In the words of George III, written for his

Young George, as Prince of Wales, grew passionately devoted to his tutor, Lord Bute. No one had ever played for George's love before.

MANSELL COLLECTION

tutor Bute in an essay while he was still Prince of Wales:

The executive power is in the prince (*that is*, Sovereign), the legislative in the nobility and the representatives of the people, and the judicial in the people and in some cases in the nobility, to whom there lies a final appeal from all other courts of judicature, where every man's life, liberty and possessions are secure, where one part of the legislative body checks the other by the privilege of rejecting, both checked by the executive, as that is again by the legislative; all parts moving, and however they may follow the particular interest of their body, yet all uniting at the last for the public good.

CHECKS AND BALANCES

What Bute added to George III's thinking was that, although the original idea had been perfect, the practice of the last forty years had sullied it. The checks and balances were not faultless *because Parliament, indulged by the Prime Minister, had arrogated excessive power*. It was the duty of the Prince of Wales,

Sam Adams, 'puritan embezzler, conspiratorial propagandist, sincere democrat and conniving back-alley politician.'

once he became King, to restore the balance by drawing back to the Throne some of the prerogatives it had surrendered through the indolence of the first two Georges; and this monarchical enterprise might even favour the admission into office of individual Tories, on the reasoning that the King was choosing advisers 'from the best men of any party'.

The second strong point which Bute impressed on George was that Great Britain should not be a 'Hanoverian' country in the sense that its foreign policy was dominated by the fate of the original Duchy of Brunswick and Luneburg, the Electorate of Hanover, which was always in territorial panic because of the danger of its being swallowed by Prussia (as it eventually was). Bute wanted no undue Continental involvement in any foreign war – such as the Seven Years War then in progress – though he would sanction an imperialist aim in that war. There must be no great European territorial aims to beat back Russia and Austria (in this particular war) for the sake of Hanover, but as much as possible might be taken from their ally, France, of her colonial possessions outside Europe.

When George III came to the throne in 1760 the Seven Years War had already achieved these imperial ambitions in North America, the West Indies and in India. The European struggle was unresolved. King George therefore acceded with the immediate intention of securing peace, and the long-term aim of regaining the lost prerogatives of the Crown.

Both were unpopular aims. Great Britain was (mistakenly) expecting further years of victory as in 1759. The London and Bristol merchants saw the prospect of more profit from war than from peace. The fact that the young King did his unpractised best to maintain his novel policies says much for Bute's tutelage, and for the pupil's character, when it is considered that the new monarch was 22 years old.

'MY DEAREST FRIEND – I WANT ADVICE'

Much of the impact can be ascribed to George's emotional attachment to the handsome Scot. In his adolescent correspondence George called Bute – not at the top of the letter but in the body of it – always 'my dearest'. A year or two later it became 'my dearest friend'. Bute unscrupulously played on this excess of affection in a sort of blackmail. George was constrained to write to him:

I am young and inexperienced and want advice. I trust in your friendship which will assist me in all difficulties. I do hope you will from this instant banish all thoughts of leaving me. I have often heard you say you don't think I shall have the same friendship for you when I am married as I now have. I shall never change in that, nor will I bear to be in the least deprived of your company.

But in the long run it was George's intellectual, rather than emotional, loyalty to Bute's tuition that counted. Though Bute was relatively soon out of office, through his own impractical inefficiency as a realistic politician, his influence was lasting on George's thinking and on the freezing of his perceptions at an adolescent level of idealistic obstinacy. These were the attitudes that displayed themselves during George III's reaction to the first two crises of his early years as King.

There were two critical issues. The first was the question of freedom of the private citizen and of the press, and the importance of the individual Member of the House of Commons, as raised by the witty debauchee, Jack Wilkes of Aylesbury, England.

The second was the question of payment for the defence of the American

Churchwarden Wilkes in 1759 held the office less by virtue of his morals than of his residence opposite St Margaret's Westminster.

MANSELL COLLECTION

colonies, leading to the subject of taxation without representation and from there to the utter worthlessness of George III to be King of America – as raised by the Puritan embezzler, conspiratorial propagandist, sincere demo-crat and conniving back-alley politician, the super-active Sam Adams of Boston, Massachusetts.

It is strange that the shadow of the honour of the King's mother hung over both these highly impersonal matters of state. But Jack Wilkes and Sam Adams could impart personality into the most theoretical subjects.

A PATRIOT BY ACCIDENT

John Wilkes was an intelligent rake who was only just a gentleman. Through his father's money and his native wit he had bought, schooled and charmed himself out of the ranks of the bourgeoisie into England's self-conscious upper class. Possibly a realisation that he had to justify his new status tempted him to be more daringly dissolute, more risqué in his witticisms, more risk-taking in that defiance of authority which – at first to

'It takes me half an hour to talk away my face.' John Wilkes, with his incurable squint.
MARY EVANS COLLECTION

his great surprise – made him the martyred champion of liberty in England and the inspiration of democratic America. 'I became a patriot by accident,' Wilkes himself once confessed. A happier accident never occurred in the best-regulated kingdom. The result was entirely beneficial. And there is no reason to doubt either the accumulative sincerity of his feelings or the effectiveness of his campaigns any more in the career of Wilkes than in the progress of other converts, from Saint Paul onwards.

His father was a London distiller who had taken advantage of a questionable royal whim and had become prosperous throughout the popularity of gin. The eighteenth-century passion of the English lower classes for gin

*Gin Alley, as seen by Hogarth. Wilkes's
father made a fortune out of the liquor.*
MARY EVANS COLLECTION

was the outcome of the deliberate trade policy of King William III, former Prince of Orange, who introduced the Dutch recipe into his new kingdom and, once the distillers had acquired the art, protected the industry by imposing heavy excise duties on French brandy, which was then its main rival. Within fifty years, as Hogarth witnessed, the gin traffic had got out of hand and King George II ordered restrictions on the trade. The thirsty mob then took to running alongside the royal coach, shouting 'No gin, no King!' Neither the traffic nor the profits were reduced to the point where the Wilkes distillery did not make a fortune, and it is ironic that, a generation later, the mob were crying, 'Wilkes and no King!'

Israel Wilkes, having made a pretty packet out of the addictive weaknesses of others, married, possibly in some sort of contrition, a severely pious nonconformist lady who long outlived him and often shook her head over the antics of her offspring. Wilkes senior was determined that his second son, John, should be brought up as a gentleman, and he gave him a good private classical education which was rounded off with a period at the University of Leyden.

BOOKS AND BAWDINESS

John Wilkes's summary of his university career might well have surprised his father (who died soon after it was completed). But it might equally possibly have gratified him simultaneously, for it was very gentlemanly. Wilkes later told James Boswell, who met him for the first time on the same day that he first called on 'the great Mr Samuel Johnson', 'I was always among women. At Leyden my father gave me as much money as I pleased. I had three or four whores and was drunk every night. Sore head the next morning, and then I read. I'm capable of sitting thirty hours over a table to study.' In this manner Wilkes developed as a felicitously well-read lecher – he collected a capacious library of books and was elected a Fellow of the Royal Society in his early twenties.

His propensity for women, and his own attractiveness to them, was complicated by an extraordinary ugliness and the devastating effect of a severe squint. 'It takes me half an hour to talk away my face,' he used to say. His talk was consistently witty and generally obscene. Boswell, himself a young man of coarse sexual tastes, left him somewhat shocked after their first meeting, noting the conversation as 'high-spirited and boisterous, rather too outrageous and profane.' The young historian Gibbon, though he paid tribute to Wilkes's 'inexhaustible spirits, infinite wit and humour, and a great deal of knowledge,' also recorded that 'he was a thorough profligate in principle as well as practice, his life stained with every vice and his conversation full of blasphemy and bawdy.'

Wilkes himself was inclined to attribute the tattered frothiness of his character to an unfortunate early marriage. The year after he came home from university, his father proposed that he should settle down in wedlock. Wilkes senior put up a family acquaintance – rich, fat, dull, Calvinist, ten years older than John. 'To please an indulgent father,' Wilkes recalled, he married this woman playing the unwilling role of 'a schoolboy dragged to the altar' – but according to his previous accounts, Wilkes was at least an experienced schoolboy. The couple were incompatible from the first, and after ten years they became legally separated. Wilkes gained the custody of their only child, Polly, to whom he was devoted through his long life. Twenty years later, after an actively erotic life, he fell hopelessly in love with a lady separated from her husband, and mourned the domesticity he could not enjoy, 'I have often sacrificed to beauty, but I never gave my heart except to you.'

THE MEDMENHAM CONNECTION

Whether an alternative Mrs Wilkes would have moulded the character of a different John Wilkes – and thus changed the course of history – is a speculative matter. The physical circumstances governing Wilkes's marriage had a decisive effect on his career. He settled in his wife's property in Aylesbury, Buckinghamshire, and enjoyed the life of a country squire. He quickly became a firm friend of the then Member of Parliament for Aylesbury, Thomas Potter, the extremely dissolute son of the late Archbishop of Canterbury (who himself was labelled 'as near an Atheist as an Archbishop can be'). Potter introduced the young Wilkes into such forms of profligacy as he had not yet encountered, but he also guided his protegé into politics.

Potter was a friend of William Pitt, the elder, who had married into the powerful Whig family of the Grenvilles, headed by Charles, Lord Temple and buttressed by Charles's brother George Grenville. At the time of Wilkes's matrimonial separation Pitt, Temple and Grenville were all ministers in the last Government of George II. Potter introduced Wilkes into this circle, where Wilkes developed not only his political ambitions but his facility for obscene versifying – and it was a combination of these

Bawdy James Boswell found John Wilkes 'rather too outrageous and profane.'
MARY EVANS COLLECTION

*Medmenham Abbey, scene of orgies
which have been 'grossly exaggerated
through ignorance and wish-fulfilment.'*
MANSELL COLLECTION

two accomplishments that were to be critical in shaping his impact on history. Potter reported to Wilkes in 1754 that, at a recent dinner with Pitt, 'We read over your Parody. He bid me tell you that he found with great concern you was as wicked and agreeable as ever.'

The influence of Potter and the Aylesbury ambiance also introduced Wilkes to Sir Francis Dashwood of West Wycombe, later a disastrous Chancellor of the Exchequer but at that time Colonel of the Buckinghamshire Militia and Father Superior of the Medmenham Monks. Wilkes was commissioned in the Militia and became a good officer. He was also elected to the latter brotherhood of a dozen rakes which included Potter, the satirist Charles Churchill, and Wilkes's crony from the Beefsteak Club, the fourth Earl of Sandwich, whose obsession with gambling without intervals for eating led to the introduction of the handy refreshment which was named after him. It was Sandwich, a longstanding but incompetent and treacherous politician who inspired the most memorable of all Wilkes's repartee. 'Wilkes,' observed the Earl, 'you shall die either of a pox or on the

*Charles Churchill, a useful poet,
roisterer and assistant editor of the*
North Briton.

gallows.' 'That depends, my lord,' Wilkes countered, 'on whether I embrace your principles or your mistress.'

THE LAUGHING PRIEST

The Medmenham Monks were an irregular congregation who assembled at Medmenham Abbey, on Dashwood's estate on the banks of the Thames between Henley and Marlow, for purposes of pleasure which had been clearly designated by Dashwood's eccentric architecture and statuary. Over the entrance to the chapter house there was carved the famous inscription on Rabelais's Abbey of Theleme, *Fay ce que couldras*: Do exactly what you will. In the garden and groves there were erotic statues with mottoes taken from the Latin poets. The Latin language, well understood then by educated persons, was extensively used to emphasise or to unveil (which is the dual role of adornment) allusions or puns considered unsuitable for un-initiated minds. Wilkes, writing the only authentic account of Medmenham Abbey, described its Priapus, 'The favourite doctrine of the Abbey was certainly not *penitence*; for in the centre of the orchard was a very grotesque figure, *and in his hand a reed stood flaming tipt with fire*, to use Milton's words, and you might trace out PENI TENTO NON PENITENTI.' The inscription, which Wilkes did not insult his readers by translating, indicated that this was a shrine dedicated to the erect penis rather than to the penitent. Wilkes continued, 'On the pedestal was a whimsical representation of Trophonius' cave, from whence all creatures were said to come out melancholy. Among that strange, dismal group, you might however remark a cock crowing and a Carmelite laughing. The words GALLVM GALLINACEVM ET SACERDOTEM GRATIS were only legible.' The reference was to the Latin proverb *Omne animal post coitum triste est, praeter gallum gallinaceum et sacerdotem gratis fornicantem* – After intercourse every being is sad except the farmyard cock and the priest who has had it for nothing.

The so-called 'Hellfire orgies' of the Medmenham Monks have been grossly exaggerated through ignorance and wish-fulfilment, and comprised little more than banqueting and fornication after the titillation of a spectacle of more public intercourse with mock-religious overtones. Sir Francis Dashwood merely had the money and the culture – and the delightful riverside surroundings of Medmenham Abbey – with which to dress up an old routine into a more theatrical occasion. The ceremony and the staging were witty and allusive, a contrived 'happening' of the 1760s with elaborately woven in-jokes. But the deliberately-leaked hints of what went on gave the known participants an agreeable aura of exoticism in the sophisticated circles where lust and envy mingled as strongly as in any other class of society.

The 4th Earl of Sandwich – always known as 'Jemmy Twitcher' after his betrayal of Wilkes.
NATIONAL PORTRAIT GALLERY

*Sir Francis Dashwood worshipping
Venus as a preliminary to his
appointment as Chancellor of the
Exchequer.*

42

By the same token, membership of the Medmenham Brotherhood gave Wilkes no excess of prestige at all in the eyes of George III, who felt, practised and displayed genuine piety. One of his first acts as King was to issue a Proclamation for the Encouragement of Piety and Virtue which made specific promises:

We do hereby declare our royal purpose and resolution to discountenance and punish all manner of vice, profaneness and immorality, particularly in such as are employed near our royal person, and we will upon all occasions distinguish persons of piety and virtue by marks of our royal favour. . . .

But George III could not in practice keep up the impetus of this impulse, and in itself the bad character of Wilkes was no grave bar to office or influence. George III was compelled to adopt with resignation a more realistic dictum that 'we must call in bad men to govern bad men,' and he even appointed the Earl of Sandwich and Sir Francis Dashwood to his Cabinet. The vital issues that promoted George's enmity with Wilkes were the politician's disparagement of the King's mother and the King's policy.

Wilkes became a member of the House of Commons in 1757. His introduction to the Grenville family had led to their adoption and encouragement of him as an able young man to be groomed for office, and Wilkes had responded with an enthusiasm understandable in someone who was not yet quite sure that he had 'arrived' in the circles of the élite. He devilled for the Grenvilles for a year or two, until they suggested that he might use some of his capital – originally in part, of course, his wife's dowry – to strike out for the vacant parliamentary seat of Berwick-on-Tweed. Wilkes made a manful effort. He ingeniously bribed the captain of a ship taking voters from London to Berwick to strand them 'by faulty navigation' in Norway. But he had had too little time and probably too little local knowledge to bribe successfully the majority of the 600 voters, and he finished with only one-third of the poll and a debit of £4000.

Three years later Potter, one of the sitting members for Aylesbury, played an accepted game of musical chairs. William Pitt, dismissed from the Government by George II, but speedily recalled as Minister at War because no one else had the calibre for the task, decided to exchange his seat at Okehampton (one of the classic rotten boroughs of Devon) for the representation of Bath. He offered his friend Potter the easy Okehampton seat. Potter took it, and offered Aylesbury to Jack Wilkes. Wilkes was returned unopposed, and Pitt publicly welcomed him to the House of Commons. But *unopposed* entry entailed the muzzling of opposition, which had cost Wilkes £7000. For that expensive outlay he could expect to sit only until the next general election, due in four years' time, or whenever the death of the sovereign should previously occur. In the event, George II died, and George III succeeded, on 25 October 1760, and Wilkes had all to do again. Within three years of the consequent election, on 20 January 1764, Wilkes was expelled from the House of Commons on the orders of George III as 'the blasphemer of his God and libeller of his King'.

FICKLE INTEGRITY

The dramatic condemnation came in the words of William Pitt, who had first favoured, then actively used this 'wicked and agreeable' fellow. Pitt, in fact, fed him with the information and incitement that made him 'the libeller of his King', but finally had proclaimed publicly in the House of Commons, 'I have no connection, association or communication with the writer.' Put not your trust in Pitt!

William Pitt demonstrated throughout his life a curious capacity for financial integrity and political fickleness, even as an architect of war, in which, like Winston Churchill, he achieved his principal fame. George II had him dismissed from the Army – he was a 28-year-old Cornet of Horse – after a parliamentary speech welcoming the marriage of the then Prince of

John Wilkes preparing an inferior issue of the North Briton. *'I wrote my best* North Briton *in bed with Betsy Green.'*

44

Wales (father of George III) which the King rightly took to be critical of the administration. Frederick Prince of Wales accordingly favoured him. Pitt, an accomplished House of Commons orator, succeeded after ten years in overcoming the King's dislike sufficiently for him to be appointed Paymaster General to the Forces. He was outstandingly successful in this post, which was considered to be the most profitable appointment in Great Britain by reason of the 'dropsy' perquisites deposited in the palm of the minister by contractors anxious to make their own exorbitant profit from selling supplies to the army and navy. Pitt refused to exact a penny of these bribes. (His son, Prime Minister for twenty years in the later part of George III's reign, was similarly incorruptible. Both the Pitts consequently contracted enormous debts, which were respectively settled by King George III and a grateful nation. It might have been more equitable to have stung the contractors.)

After nine years of office Pitt the elder hoped to succeed to the position of Leader of the House of Commons. But, when he was not appointed, he attacked the government from the Government Front Bench. George II accordingly dismissed him. At the same time King George reluctantly agreed to the appointment of the Earl of Bute as political adviser to his daughter-in-law, the widowed Augusta Princess of Wales, and to her son, the heir to the throne, George Prince of Wales.

PROFITABLE WAR-MAKER

Bute immediately entered into an alliance with Pitt. The Seven Years War was brewing, and both Pitt and Bute were adamantly resolved that British effort and expenditure should not be poured out within Europe to support Frederick the Great of Prussia against the onslaught of the French, even if the sustenance of Prussia spelt the (temporary) security of Hanover. But when Pitt was recalled to lead the government jointly with the Duke of Newcastle and to take on the Ministry of War, he reversed his policy and maintained Frederick with heavy subsidies derived from taxation within Great Britain. At the same time the well-equipped and highly professional Royal Navy, using its powers of blockade, transport and battle force, enabled the profitable colonial wars to be won in America, India, Africa and the Caribbean.

The Seven Years War was virtually won during the period 1758–1760, apart from the fruits of the five rich Caribbean islands which were to fall later as a result of the British naval supremacy that had already been

*The Battle of San Domingo. Three
English ships fought five French vessels
and captured four of them, three weeks
before George III ascended the throne.*

established. Pitt was the acknowledged architect of victory. On 25 October 1760 George III succeeded to the throne at the age of 22. Bute was his powerful adviser. Bute and the King were now fiercely antagonistic to Pitt, and as a corollary to that personal enmity they wanted to end the heavy financial strain of the prolonged war. In hindsight they may be credited with much reason on their side. But a swift peace was not what Pitt wanted, not what the City of London wanted, nor what was wanted by a member of Parliament who was beginning to be noticed as a minor spokesman both for Pitt and the City of London – John Wilkes.

George II died at 7.30 in the morning. By six o'clock in the evening King George III was making his accession speech to the Privy Council. Bute had written it in advance. The last sentence ran:

As I mount the throne in the midst of a bloody and expensive war, I shall endeavour to prosecute it in the manner most likely to bring an honourable and lasting peace.

Pitt listened and was enraged. He immediately cornered Bute in protest.

He saw the reference to the war as derogatory to himself, and the intentions expressed on peace-making as a verbal abandonment of Great Britain's ally, Frederick the Great of Prussia, who had contained French armed forces, supported by £2½ million which Pitt had given him in subsidies, and who, after bearing the weight of four years' continental attrition, needed more time to regain lost territory. After an angry discussion with Bute which lasted two hours, and a sulky reconsideration by the King which lasted much longer, the King's Speech was formally published as having announced:

As I mount the throne in the midst of an *expensive, but just and necessary* war, I shall endeavour to prosecute it in the manner most likely to bring an honourable and lasting peace *in concert with our Allies*.

At the request of Russia, Pitt began negotiations for peace with France, Russia and Austria, but without ceasing to make war – and through this policy he gained the bargaining counters of Dominica in the West Indies, Pondicherry in India, and Belle Ile in metropolitan France. But the French negotiators began to drag their feet. France had, in fact, made a secret treaty which would bring Spain into the war on her side. Fully aware of this arrangement, Pitt proposed to declare war on Spain before the autumn arrival of her treasure-fleet from South America, which would finance many months of belligerency. The King rejected this proposal, and Pitt could find no support in the Cabinet except from his brother-in-law Charles, Lord Temple, the patron of John Wilkes.

THE GALLEONS UNLOAD

Pitt accordingly resigned, and Temple went with him. The Spanish waited until their treasure-galleons were in port, and then declared war on Great Britain – which was badly judged, since the British captured Havana in the West Indies and Manila in the Philippines. Bute pushed through the Cabinet King George's proposal to end the subsidy to Prussia, and in the ensuing shambles of resignation he became Prime Minister himself. He recognised almost immediately that he was incapable of the man-management necessary to control the unruly House of Commons factions. But an end to the 'bloody and expensive' war had been forced.

A peace treaty was finally negotiated between May and November 1762, and it was submitted to Parliament in December. Bute had now called in as Leader of the House of Commons the most cynical and corrupt of all

A British invasion of France at Saint Cast beaten off by the French in the Seven Years War.

MARY EVANS COLLECTION

48

parliamentary manipulators, Henry Fox. Although, in the debate, Pitt declaimed dramatically against acceptance of the peace treaty, the King's Government put all possible pressure on parliamentary pensioners and placemen, and the terms were approved by 319 votes to 65.

In effect, Bute had won the day. In fact, the triumph was the King's, for Bute was already faltering as a resolute minister. To be just, the vote on the peace was not a remarkably unpopular victory in regard to its *matter*. Many in Great Britain recognised that the country could not afford the prolongation of the war, although it was generally felt that the British negotiators had given far too much away. But it was highly unpopular for the *manner* in which it had been achieved – not because of the arm-twisting practised by Fox, but because of the apparent dominance of Bute. As Fox shrewdly summed up the confrontation, opposition to the peace was directed 'against the man, not the measure'.

FROM SCOTLAND, BUT COULD NOT HELP IT

Bute was popularly hated with a virulence that was irrational. On the day of George's accession Bute had made it plain to the leaders of the Government, Pitt and the Duke of Newcastle, that he was to be the King's oracle. Two days later he was appointed to the Cabinet. Four months later he became Secretary of State. The Establishment sulkily observed his manner and suspiciously analysed his motives covering all his actions from the accession. But a more general abhorrence among the influential southern middle classes and the mob took longer to develop. There were, however, two counts on his charge-sheet from the beginning. The first was that his name and origins were Scottish. As a Stuart he was in fact descended from a bastard line of the Kings of Scotland, but it was unfortunate that the 'legitimate' line of Stuarts had been the leaders, and would-be kings, of the armed rebellions of 1715 and 1745 which had put England into memorable panic.

Nowadays we treat with some amusement the blunt remarks loosed off by men as educated as Dr Johnson against the Scots. They were more serious observations at the time. Boswell, who had already taken lessons in English elocution, said falteringly at his first meeting with Dr Johnson, 'Indeed, I come from Scotland, but I cannot help it.' It was a defence not uttered lightly. Even Johnson, a propagandist for and pensioner of King George III, wrote with objective disparagement of his monarch that, when he came to the throne, 'he had long been in the hands of the Scots'.

Ordinary people peered at events in an endeavour to see some trace of undue Scottish influence on the new King, emanating from Bute as his eminence grise. Curiously, they found it almost immediately, and this was the second indictment of Bute. It arose in a phrase from the King's first speech to Parliament which later historians have praised for its significance on an entirely different level. George's father, the dead Prince of Wales, left a testament for his son which counselled him, 'Convince this nation that you are not only an Englishman born and bred, but that you are also this by inclination.' George III told his first Parliament, 'Born and educated in this country, I glory in the name of Britain.'

THE NAME OF ENGLISHMAN

This was an apparently unexceptional remark which has since become legendary. But the Duke of Newcastle and many others at the time took strong exception to it. They seized on the word *Britain*, objecting to its implication that it conveyed an over-emphasis on Scotland. Newcastle said, 'It denotes the author to all the world,' meaning that Bute had written the speech. Even in 1769 Junius was writing to the King, 'When you affectedly renounced the name of Englishman, believe me, Sir, you were persuaded

Bute, emerging from the Boot, showers
gold on all his fellow Scots in a caricature
of 1762.
MANSELL COLLECTION

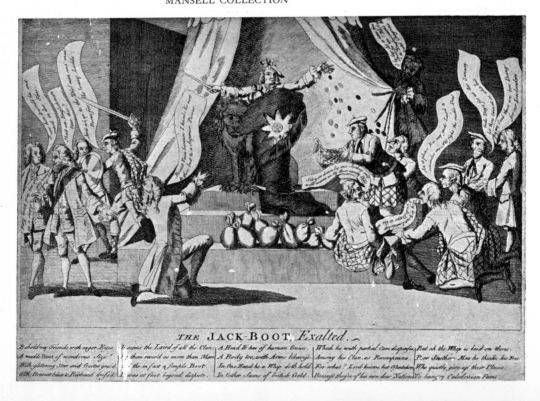

THE JACK-BOOT, *Exalted.*

THE
LETTERS OF JUNIUS.
VOL. I.

IOHN WILKES.
Member of Parliament for Aylesb...

Great without Title, beyond Fortu...
Rich even when plunder'd, honour'd...
Lov'd without Youth, & follow'd wit...
At Home, tho'exil'd, free, tho'in th...

I. Miller del. et Sculp.   Publ. acc. to the Act June 30 1763.

John Wilkes: his connection with Junius
remained unestablished.

*Bute was reputed to be a power behind
the throne long after his hasty retirement.
This drawing satirises our Ambassador
in Paris as one of his minions,
receiving instructions in 1774.*
MARY EVANS COLLECTION

to pay a very ill-judged compliment to one part of your subjects at the expense of another.'

Strangely, the only parallel, which might have given the critics some justification was the first speech of Queen Anne, made to delegations of both houses of Parliament within hours of her accession to the throne in 1702:

As I know my own heart to be entirely English, I can very sincerely assure you that there is not anything you can expect or desire from me which I shall not be ready to do for the happiness and prosperity of England.

Anne vocally emphasised the word *English* in the beautiful voice which had been trained by a Drury Lane actress. But she was speaking on the day of the death of the 'passionate Dutchman', her unpopular predecessor King William III, and she was addressing an English Parliament. It was five

years before the Act of Union, which merged the Parliament of Scotland
into the assembly at Westminster.

BOOT AND PETTICOAT

Bute had been the consistent target of scurrilous abuse by mob demonstrations, pamphlets and political cartoons, since he had emerged as the
political adviser to Augusta and Prince George, some years before the
Accession. The symbols of his supposed depravity were generally the Boot
and the Petticoat, carried on staves for ultimate burning during many a
public riot, to portray the (false) charge of adultery between Bute and the
Princess of Wales. Young George did not escape this obloquy. A caricature
of 1757 depicts him, wearing the star and ribbon of the Garter, with Bute,
and it spells out their identities in the rhyming caption:

> *See a blue riband, silly proud son of a Whore.*
> *See a strutting Scotch peer, of whom I could say more.*

The campaign against Bute naturally intensified when he came into office
as King George's minister. It rose to climaxes of mob fury after Pitt had

George III as portrayed by the French.
MANSELL COLLECTION

been squeezed out of the government before the Spanish war, and on the eve of the approval by Parliament of the mild peace terms offered a year later. There is no doubt that these violent demonstrations were engineered by powerful men in the City of London who had profited from the war and would lose by a 'weak' peace treaty which restored rich trading territory to France and Spain. On Lord Mayor's day 1761 the City invited not only the King and Bute to the Guildhall banquet, but also the ousted Pitt and Temple. While Pitt was acclaimed with an ovation, the King was insulted at dinner and Bute cowered white-faced after a mob attack on his coach which would have led to serious injury if his own hired bodyguards had not joined the battle. Investigation showed that Lord Mayor Beckford had personally visited public houses over the previous night to appoint ringleaders of mob action. At the State Opening of Parliament in 1762, the King was booed but Bute was hissed and pelted by the mob, who would have overturned his coach and got to physical grips with him if the Guards had not been called in to the rescue.

At the Gordon Riots Wilkes fired on his own supporters.
MARY EVANS COLLECTION

John Wilkes inevitably became involved in this conflict. He was the legman and stringer for Pitt and Temple. He had an innate sympathy, possibly not immediately realised, for the City of London merchants. But City magnates were mocked by the educated classes from 1700 to 1900 as rich, self-made, ill-bred incubi; and even Wilkes, with a father of the same mould, could not resist the occasional temptation to dig at their faulty grammar – the general mockery subsided only when the magnates sent their sons to public schools and brought them into the business. But the spread of upper class accent did not guarantee a continuity of the first class business brain which the City merchants had previously depended on for success.

Wilkes, as a manufacturer's son who had been bought the rank of gentleman, intelligently exploited the friction he perceived between the political aims of the King and the City, but did not crawl the pubs to drum up support. He was not a manipulator of mobs. Mobs embarrassed him, even when they were demonstrating for him. And, twenty years later, as Alderman during the Gordon Riots, he fired on rioters wearing his own cockade, and saved the Bank of England and much of Fleet Street from destruction. Wilkes's forte was not in intimidation, but in persuasion, propaganda through the printed word, scurrilous but witty, inciting because incisive. Wilkes therefore played his part in the campaign against the 'shameful peace' and its instigators, King George III and Lord Bute, by going into print. This was the beginning of his becoming 'a patriot by accident'. He was not then conducting a profound offensive. It was an opportunist foray which appealed to his sense of mischief. His fencing was skilful, but not without frivolity. It was the repression he provoked that set him on the crusade for liberty.

OPPOSE, EXPOSE, DEPOSE

Wilkes took up pamphleteering and unsigned journalism directed against the proposed peace treaty – 'surely it is the peace of God, for it passeth all understanding,' he was the first to say. His earliest publication was *Observations on the Papers relative to the Rupture with Spain*, a pamphlet for which he was briefed by Pitt. He contributed effectively to an anti-government newspaper called *The Monitor* whose editorial aim was succinctly expressed as 'To oppose and expose and depose.' On 29 May 1762 Bute became Prime Minister after days of anxious irresolution and well-founded

doubt about his adequacy for the post. He had determined to promote some propaganda support, and he had hired in advance to edit a pro-Government newspaper a fellow Scot, Tobias Smollet, who at the age of 41 had then written all his novels except *Humphrey Clinker*.

The new paper was called *The Briton* (thus giving some support in passing to Newcastle's theory about the authorship of George III's first speech to Parliament). *The Briton* first appeared as a weekly paper on the day Bute took office. Seven days later, on 5 June 1762, a rival paper appeared. It was called *The North Briton*, and was written mainly by John Wilkes with assistance from the satirical poets Charles Churchill and Robert Lloyd. *The Briton* was a pro-Government paper – *The North Briton* was very decidedly not. *The Briton*, with a circulation struggling towards 250, was not a runaway success. *The North Briton* strode swiftly to take and hold a circulation of 2000 copies a week. Wilkes's newspaper derived its name from a satirical reference to its rival. Wilkes instituted the fiction that it was written by an over-enthusiastic Scot who made appalling *gaffes* through his naive adulation of Lord Bute. But this necessity for double-take of *double-entendre* blunted the edge of the writer's destructive wit and was speedily abandoned.

Indeed, in much of his writing Wilkes was from the very beginning entirely direct and unequivocal in the impetus of his attack. The first article of his first number started nobly, even prophetically:

The liberty of the press is the birthright of a Briton and is justly esteemed the firmest bulwark of the liberties of this country. It has been the terror of all bad ministers; for their dark and dangerous designs, or their weakness, inability and duplicity, have thus been detected and shewn to the public, generally in too strong and just colours for them long to bear up against the odium of mankind . . . A wicked and corrupt administration must naturally dread this appeal to the world; and will be for keeping all the means of information equally from the prince, parliament and people. Every method will then be try'd, and all parts put in practice to check the spirit of knowledge and enquiry. Even the courts of justice have in the most dangerous way, because under the sanction of law, been drawn in to second the dark views of an arbitrary ministry, and to stifle in the birth all infant virtue.

Wilkes then proceeded to name names and to particularise cases. The fur began to fly from the first number of his paper.

HIS LORDSHIP LOST HIS NERVE

Lord Temple, who had left the government at the same time as his brother-in-law, Pitt, had been the principal agent in launching *The North Briton* and in getting Wilkes to edit it. After two issues, in which Bute had been very severely lambasted, Temple lost his nerve and asked Wilkes to stop publication. The violence of the philippic invective frightened him, and he was particularly disturbed to read 'Lord Bute's name at full length' when

Hogarth, always opposed to Wilkes and Churchill, drew this satirical study of 'The Bruiser C. Churchill (once the Revd.) in the character of a modern Hercules, regaling himself after having killed the monster Caricatura [that is, Hogarth] that so sorely galled his virtuous friend, the Heaven-born Wilkes.' The mourning dog is Hogarth's.

at that time most pamphlet propaganda skated hopefully away from a libel action by printing 'Lord B——'.

Only three issues of the paper had in fact been scheduled and financed, and a timid editor might have stopped when support was withdrawn. Wilkes, however, had the bit between his teeth and a high circulation to justify his dominance of the situation. He politely declined to cease publication. To do Temple justice, he did not withdraw his distant approval, nor his political support, nor, when disaster struck, personal finance to keep Wilkes solvent. And it was, in fact, the passing over by Temple to Wilkes hard news of future policy which had been leaked to him – together with Pitt's expert advice on how to use that leak – which produced the climactic No. 45.

Meanwhile Wilkes amused himself with facetious satire at the general expense of the Scots, before producing his first blockbuster. The public reaction was already sensational. After four issues a London clubman remarked, 'Mr Wilkes may be very mild and smooth in his private address, but his public addresses are as rough as a bear's arse.' Wilkes proceeded to get even rougher with No. 5 of *The North Briton*, dated 3 July 1762. It was with this issue that King George III took his first active personal interest in Wilkes.

KING GEORGE FEELS THE LASH

The theme was not a new one in the polemics of that time. The treatment, however, was startlingly savage. The subject was taken from English history. Roger Mortimer, later first Earl of March, was the lover of Queen Isabella ('She-Wolf of France'), the wife of King Edward II. Edward imprisoned Mortimer in the Tower, but Isabella contrived his escape and fled to France to be with him, virtually kidnapping her son, the heir to the throne. Mortimer and Isabella invaded England and forced the abdication of Edward II, later murdering him in one of the most sordid acts of English history. Isabella's son succeeded as Edward III, a lad of fourteen under the control of his mother and her lover. Isabella and Mortimer signed humiliating treaties with France and Scotland renouncing Edward's rights there. The King's uncles resisted, but their opposition was not co-ordinated, and the Queen and her lover executed one of them. However, at the age of 16, already married and a father, Edward III called a Parliament at Nottingham, penetrated the Castle at night with a few friends, plucked Mortimer out of his mother's bed, and had him hanged at Tyburn as an enemy of the State.

*Bute and Augusta in the centre of a
lively dance supported by Chatham, right,
Townshend, left, with Wilkes above en
route to Paris.*

Isabella was confined for the 28 remaining years of her life in Castle Rising
in Norfolk. Edward III reigned for half a century, 'happy and glorious',
as one of the most glamorous Kings of England.

The opportunism of a wicked adaptation of the theme of Isabella,
Mortimer and Edward III to the situation of Augusta, Bute and George
III was irresistibly tempting. The insinuations which could be drawn were
sharp. Wilkes etched in every one of them with acid. King George had
truly mortifying matter to read on that first weekend in July. Even the
minor details of the historic narrative applied to him. He too, like Edward,
had just become a father for the first time.

George III as Gainsborough saw him.
MANSELL COLLECTION

INSOLENT FAVOURITE

King George read a disarming introductory paragraph on the subject of court favourites before reaching the passage in which Wilkes showed his hand and his cunning. He was to discuss the happiness of a kingdom and the honour due to a King where that King had had the greatness of heart to banish the favourite. But Wilkes left himself a sufficiency of space in which first to speak scurrilously of the favourite:

Examples of successful virtue prove generally stronger incentives to glorious actions. It may therefore perhaps be more expedient, instead of painting the miseries which a country must be involved in if governed by an insolent *favourite*, to shew the peculiar felicity of a prince and people rescued from the tyrannous slavery of a *court minion*, exemplified in the deliverance of this country by the noble and manly conduct of Edward the Third.

His father had favourites and he was deposed. His people were not freed from fears of falling into a more dreaded situation. They knew what the government of a weak and imprudent King could do, but they were unexperienced as to the effects of a minority under the direction of a *Mother*, actuated by strong passions and influenced by an insolent minister.

Mortimer, afterwards Earl of March, was, through the ascendancy he had obtained over the Queen Mother, in fact the sole Regent. At his pleasure the great officers of state were appointed or removed; he assumed the authority of the King, and solely possessed his ear: the King's uncles, the president of the regency and the whole nobility were not suffered to approach their sovereign unless their opinions coincided with Mortimer's; and in their intercourse, only permitted in this manner, care was taken to have his Majesty so surrounded by spies that the minister could not fail to receive information of every measure intended to injure him in the opinion of the King. Thus educated under the guidance of his *Mother*, thus secured by the custody of Mortimer, he was easily persuaded to believe that Mortimer was a faithful friend and a consummate minister.

Wilkes detailed some of the history of the invasion of England by Robert the Bruce, and Mortimer's subsequent betrayal of Edward's military victory over the Scot:

A shameful peace was concluded for him by the influence of Mortimer, such a peace as, historians say, was profitable to the Queen Mother and Mortimer, but inconsistent with the honour of the King and the profit of the realm and people.

Wilkes then examined the evidence that Mortimer and Isabella were indeed adulterous lovers:

Historians scruple not to affirm that, as Mortimer was endebted for the enormity of his power to a criminal correspondence with the Queen Mother, so to honest insinuations of this given to the King must be ascribed his amazing downfall.

In a disingenuous effort to appear to present the case for the Queen's defence, Wilkes mischievously emphasised the resemblances between the guilty lovers of a past age and the Augusta and Bute of the day. He quoted the plea in mitigation of the historian Barnes:

Surely whoever considers the inequality of the Queen's age with that of Mortimer's, she being little more than thirty, and he at least more than fifty, will rather believe that by his subtle and crafty insinuations he made himself necessary to the Queen's councils, than that his person could ever render him acceptable to her bed; she herself being accounted one of the most delicate ladies of the age: whereas he was not only a married man, but the father of eleven children.

Yet, Wilkes, was compelled to report, Mortimer was impeached for his sexual relationship with the Queen:

If it had not been notorious, there is no likelihood that the parliament would have wounded the princess's honour so deeply, which could not but reflect on the King her son.

That passage, above all others, must have rekindled in King George III the flame of the oath he had taken, 'I do therefore here in the presence of Our Almighty Lord promise that I will ever remember the insults done to my mother, and never will forgive anyone who shall offer to speak disrespectfully of her.' But Wilkes had not finished with him. The writer summarised the physical events of Edward seizing Mortimer in the presence of the Queen Mother, sending him to the Tower, taking over the Government himself, and assenting to the execution of the favourite. Then he uttered his damning pseudo-pious hopes for the present:

O may Britain never see such a day again! when power acquired by profligacy may lord it over this realm; when the feeble pretensions of a *court minion* may require the prostitution of royalty for their support.

YOU WILL NEVER BE FORGIVEN

The Town – that is, fashionable and political London – read No. 5 of *The North Briton* with shocked delight. 'The prostitution of royalty' was indeed a phrase to be repeated behind the raised fan or the opened snuff-box, in whichever of its possible references it could be interpreted – and the paper had skilfully left such interpretation to the reader. Charles Churchill reported to Wilkes with trembling glee, 'The paper will never be forgotten, and you will never be forgiven, as it is universally ascribed to you. It has opened the eyes of many. "Hated by knaves and knaves to hate" may not be your motto, but will undoubtedly be your fate through life. I desire you to take great care of your health, and still more of your life.'

The life of John Wilkes was indeed to be put in danger, because of his writings in *The North Briton*, twice at the hands of the King's Friends. On both occasions the medium was duelling. The first was a hot-tempered affair of so-called 'honour'. The second occurrence bore and still bears the indications of a carefully-rehearsed attempt to murder, although not done with the connivance of the King.

The affair of honour involved the Lord Steward of the King's Household, a young and rather clumsy peer called Lord Talbot. Talbot had had a variety of traditional duties to perform in the ceremonial at the King's Coronation Banquet, and had bungled every one. His most ridiculous *gaffe* was over a manoeuvre which he had thought up for himself. At the beginning of the banquet it was customary that he should enter Westminster Hall on horseback leading the long line of servants who were carrying the dishes of the first course. Talbot decided that his exit should be as unforgettable as his entry – and indeed he succeeded in this. He had been inspired by the idea of making his horse retire backwards, keeping the rider's face always turned towards the King. He set himself to train his horse, and many courtiers were agog to see this impressive feat of dressage. Unfortunately, Talbot's horse mixed up his cues, and insisted on progressing backwards all the way up Westminster Hall to the royal table, after which he walked out normally, thus presenting his and Talbot's hind-quarters to the King for the whole of the ceremony. Wilkes made a humorous comment on this memorable performance in *The North Briton*, and Talbot immediately wrote to him to confirm that he was the writer. Wilkes replied that Talbot had no right to ask this question. Talbot challenged Wilkes to a duel at the Red Lion Inn at Bagshot. Wilkes said he would attend for supper with Talbot and fight him in the morning, and he rode over from Medmenham carrying sword and pistols – a generous gesture since, as the man challenged, he had choice of weapons and was much more skilful with the sword. At Bagshot Talbot refused to sit at table with Wilkes, and again demanded whether Wilkes had written the in-sulting reference in *The North Briton*. Wilkes said that Lord Talbot would

Medmenham Abbey, from which, after a heavy night, Wilkes rode to Bagshot for the duel with Lord Talbot.
MANSELL COLLECTION

Boswell shared 'wine and punch in plenty and freedom' at the Beefsteak Club with John Wilkes.
MARY EVANS COLLECTION

have to prove his right to catechise Wilkes about a paper that did not bear his name, adding that Wilkes's conception of liberty was 'that I obeyed with pleasure a gracious sovereign, but would never submit to the arbitrary dictates of a fellow-subject.'

THE WORLD WILL CONCLUDE I AM DRUNK

Talbot insisted on fighting that night, and with pistols. Wilkes said: 'I am come from Medmenham Abbey, where the jovial monks of St Francis kept me up till four in the morning. The world will conclude that I am drunk, and will form no favourable opinion of your lordship from a duel at such a time. Nevertheless, I will fight you for all that, although I know that your lordship fights me with the King's Pardon in your pocket, while I fight you with a halter round my neck. If you fall, I cannot tarry here a moment for the tender mercies of the present Ministry, but must immediately flee to France; and this I have arranged to do.'

Wilkes wrote a farewell letter giving Temple instructions for the education of his daughter Polly. At seven in the evening, in bright moonlight, the two men and their seconds walked to a garden some distance from the inn. They had agreed not to turn round, but to face each other until they fired. They used Wilkes's powder and bullets and Talbot's large horse-pistols. Wilkes's second gave the word, and they fired. Both shots missed, and Wilkes immediately walked up to Talbot and admitted that he had

64

GEORG..

G. Kneller.
Eqᵗ pinx.

*George 1 (1660–1727) who reigned from
1714 to 1727. He was once the Elector
of Hanover and, disliking England, spent
as much time as possible there.*

George II (1683–1760) was on the
throne from 1727 to 1760. Like his
predecessor, George I, Hanover was
preferred to England. George II was the
last English king to lead his troops into
battle, at Rettinger in 1743.

written the passage in the paper. Talbot said he was a brave and noble fellow, and asked him to go back to the inn to drink a bottle of claret. 'Which we did,' Wilkes recalled, 'with great good humour and much laughter.'

The second duel in which Wilkes was engaged arose from the far more serious campaign which *The North Briton* was constantly pressing against the 'shameful peace' and the corruption attending its preliminaries and consequencies. The conspiracy – if, as Horace Walpole and other contemporaries believed, it was indeed 'a plot against the life of Wilkes' – took eight months to hatch, and resulted in the wounded Wilkes being absent from the Commons at the time of his expulsion. In the meantime, more juridical schemes were being prepared against him.

THE GENERAL WARRANT

In November 1762 the Government issued a general warrant – that is, an order to arrest persons described through their occupations, but not named – against the authors, printers and publishers of *The Monitor*, the anti-Government paper for which Wilkes had written before he founded *The North Briton*. Wilkes proposed to Arthur Beardmore, the editor of *The Monitor*, that they should jointly test the legality of a general warrant by openly resisting it. This was a proposition of some weight, since the House of Commons had impeached Lord Chief Justice Scroggs for issuing general warrants during the anti-Catholic terror campaign following the panic engineered by Titus Oates in 1678. But Beardmore would not undertake the strain of such a confrontation with the Government. Instead, he admitted his authorship and submitted to the substitution of a special warrant which named him. The consequence was that *The Monitor* was suppressed.

Almost immediately the Government seized its tactical advantage and issued a general warrant against 'the authors, printers and publishers of a seditious and scandalous weekly paper entitled *The North Briton*, beginning with Number One and ending with Number Twenty-five.' Wilkes defied this *lettre de cachet* by refusing to admit his authorship, and immediately publishing No. 26 of the *North Briton*.

It was a purely legalistic ploy, because 'everybody who was anybody' knew that he had written *The North Briton*. On the day of publication of No. 26, when Wilkes dined at the Beefsteak Club (the 'Sublime Society of Beefsteaks', with premises in a room at the top of Covent Garden Theatre),

SANDWICH-CARROTS! dainty SANDWICH-CARROTS.

Expelled from the Beefsteak Club, the
Earl of Sandwich was reduced to
groping in Bond Street.

MARY EVANS COLLECTION

Boswell happened to be a guest, only a fortnight after his arrival in London. In a unique description of the proceedings he casually named Wilkes as 'author of *The North Briton*':

The president sits in a chair under a canopy, above which you have in golden letters, *Beef and Liberty*. We were entertained by the Club. Lord Sandwich was in the chair, a jolly, hearty, lively man. It was a very mixed society, Lord Eglinton [a friend of Bute's], Mr Beard [John Beard, actor, singer and manager of Covent Garden Theatre, for whom some of Handel's finest tenor parts were expressly composed], Colonel West of the Guards, Mr Havard the actor, Mr Churchill the poet, Mr Wilkes the author of *The North Briton*, and many more. We had nothing to eat but beefsteaks, and had wine and punch in plenty and freedom. We had a number of songs.

In some uncertainty over Wilkes's jaunty rebuff, the Government withdrew the general warrant. But the action had had the effect – which can similarly be seen today in difficulties over the production of outspoken papers like *Private Eye* – of scaring off the printers. The original printer withdrew. The next printer lost his nerve after one issue and resigned the contract. Wilkes found another printer and rode the storm serenely. He wrote in the next issue of *The North Briton*:

Almost every man I meet looks strangely on me. Some industriously avoid me – others pass me by silent – stare – and shake their heads. Those few, those very few, who are not afraid to take a lover of his country by the hand, congratulate me on being alive and at Liberty. They advise circumspection – for, they do not know – they cannot tell – but – the times – Liberty is precious – fines – imprisonment – pillory – not indeed that they themselves think – but – then in truth – God only knows . . .

REVENGE RESERVED

The North Briton went on its way, challenging, provoking. After Parliament's final approval of the peace terms, Wilkes turned to other scandals of the day, while still pressing his attack on Bute. The reward for the managers inside Parliament who had had the influence to convert a doubtful balance of Commons votes into a landslide in favour of Bute's treaty was, said *The North Briton*, £350,000. It was found by ear-marking ten per cent of a new Government loan of £3½ million, and it was principally distributed by Samuel Martin, Secretary to the Treasury and a Member of Parliament whom the paper described – giving evidence to justify most of the adjec-

*Sir Francis Dashwood, Chancellor of
the Exchequer, after 'puzzling all his
life over tavern bills'.*
MANSELL COLLECTION

tives – as 'the most treacherous, base, selfish, mean, abject, lowlived and dirty fellow that ever wriggled himself into a secretaryship'. Samuel Martin writhed, and reserved his revenge for a more opportune occasion, as did another of Wilkes's butts, his old friend Sir Francis Dashwood, who had introduced an incomprehensible excise tax on cider.

In spite of his known position as presiding Abbot of the Medmenham Monks, Dashwood had been accepted by the King as his Chancellor of the Exchequer. It was an elevation which surprised no one more than Dashwood, of whom it was said, 'A figure of five digits was an incomprehensible mystery'. Wilkes wrote of him, 'From puzzling all his life over tavern bills, he was called by Lord Bute to administer the finances of a kingdom above one hundred million in debt.' But Dashwood himself had cheerfully written to Wilkes, 'I think I am equally fit to be head of the Church as of the Exchequer.'

Wilkes returned to the theme of Bute as a latter-day Mortimer. This second attack appeared, not in *The North Briton*, but in an essay which he wrote anonymously (though the authorship was never in doubt) as a satirical introduction to a reprint of an old play, *The Fall of Mortimer*, which was published ten days after his attack on Martin and four days before his ridicule of Dashwood. Wilkes dedicated the play to 'the Right Honourable John Earl of Bute', but he declared that his principal motive for 'making this humble offering to the shrine of Bute' was because of his lordship's accomplishments as an actor. (Bute had, in fact, most deeply ingratiated himself with Frederick, Prince of Wales after their first meeting because of their mutual interest in amateur theatricals.) Wilkes therefore denied any suggestion that he was drawing a parallel between the actions, in bed or in the council chamber, of Bute and Mortimer:

Samuel Martin, MP, 'the most mean, abject, lowlived and dirty fellow that ever wriggled himself into a secretaryship', had his revenge on Wilkes by wounding him in a contrived duel.
MARY EVANS COLLECTION

I have felt an honest indignation at all the invidious and odious applications of the story of Roger Mortimer. I absolutely disclaim the most distant allusion, and I purposely dedicate this play to your lordship, because history does not furnish a more striking contrast thàn there is between the two ministers in the reigns of Edward the Third and George the Third.

Wilkes therefore devoted himself to Bute's acting. But the Prime Minister could find little comfort in his praise:

In another part you were no less perfect; I mean in that familiar scene in *Hamlet*, where you *pour fatal poison into the ear* of a good, unsuspecting king.

ODIOUS AND CONTEMPTIBLE

At this point of time, though Wilkes did not then know it, he had won. The crushing of Bute as Prime Minister, though not necessarily yet as eminence grise, had been achieved. From the middle of March 1763 George III knew that his 'dearest friend' was adamant on resignation, though the announcement was not made for some weeks. The campaign therefore continued. In No. 44 of *The North Briton*, published on 2 April 1763, Wilkes indulged in his strongest invective:

The restless and turbulent disposition of the Scottish nation before the Union, with their constant attachment to France and declared enmity to England, their repeated perfidies and rebellions since that period, with their servile behaviour in time of need, and overbearing insolence in power, have justly rendered the very name of Scot hateful to every Englishman. The mean arts by which the present minister acquired his power, and his conduct since the acquisition of it, the long and dark scenes of dissimulation which he ran through for the sake of greatness, with the open and insolent outrages he hath committed since his accession to it against men much better than himself, the little capacity which he hath shewn for business; his contempt for the English nobles, especially of those who are known and tried friends of the Constitution, and his strict union with those who are the avowed enemies of it . . . these things laid together have rendered the minister justly suspected by the people, and have, if possible, made the name of *Stuart* more odious and contemptible than it was before.

TO PARIS WITH POLLY

Wilkes now sensed that his task was done and that Bute was finished. He went off to Paris with his daughter Polly, now thirteen years old, to install her in a finishing school, and also to have a better opportunity of seducing

Madame de Pompadour. 'How far does freedom of the Press extend in England?' she asked Wilkes. 'That, Madame,' he replied, 'is what I am trying to find out.'
MARY EVANS COLLECTION

her governess, Madame Carpentier. He arrived to find that his reputation, both as an agitator and a profligate, had preceded him. 'How far does freedom of the press extend in England?' he was asked by Madame de Pompadour, the extremely capable and intellectual mistress of King Louis XV. 'That, Madame, is what I am trying to find out,' Wilkes replied. But, characteristically, he made a swift retreat from pretentiousness, and bent his mind to seduction. 'Dissipation and profligacy renew the mind,' he assured James Boswell. 'I wrote my best *North Briton* in bed with Betsy Green.'

Bute formally resigned as Prime Minister on 9 April 1763. But there was an entire absence of any indication that he had ceased to be the King's backstairs adviser. He saw George constantly in private. Wilkes had been prepared to discontinue *The North Briton* from the moment of the change of ministry, and no issue appeared for two weeks. But he hurried back from France to tackle the new situation. He conferred with Lord Temple, who had been discussing affairs with William Pitt, and confirmed his disquiet.

73

W. Ridley sculp.!

Almost immediately an event occurred which led to the writing and publication of that historic issue of *The North Briton*, No. 45.

CONTINUE THE CRUSADE

By a fateful coincidence, Bute had been succeeded as Prime Minister by George Grenville, the brother of Temple and brother-in-law of Pitt, though the two latter were not included in the ministry. Grenville needed advice on a parliamentary tactic, and sent to his brother Temple an advance copy of the King's Speech which was to be made at the end of the parliamentary session on Tuesday 19 April. From the terms of the speech it seemed clear that, in relation not only to the aftermath of peace and to policies of national economy but, far more seriously, with regard to the powers claimed by the Crown, Bute's policy was not being watered down, but mightily strengthened. Temple accordingly decided that *The North Briton*'s crusade against the King's Government must not be abandoned with the resignation of Bute, but intensified. He consulted Pitt on the broader political lines of the necessary campaign. There is no clear evidence that Pitt and Wilkes conferred on this occasion, but Temple certainly briefed Wilkes after his conference with Pitt. As a result, Wilkes wrote the clearest argument yet advanced in that age regarding the growing power of the Crown. He skilfully avoided direct criticism of the King by inveighing against the insolence of the ministers who had put their words into his mouth. But it was a ploy that did nothing to divert the fury of either George III or his Cabinet. The explosive issue of *The North Briton* appeared on Saint George's Day, 23 April 1763.

The pugilism began with one formal feint, followed by a succession of knockdown punches:

The King's Speech has always been considered by the legislature, and by the public at large, as the *Speech of the Minister* . . . This week has given the public the most abandoned instance of ministerial effrontery ever attempted to be imposed on mankind. The *minister's speech* of last Tuesday is not to be paralleled in the annals of this country. I am in doubt whether the imposition is greater on the sovereign or on the nation. Every friend of his country must lament that a prince of so many great and amiable qualities, whom England truly reveres, can be brought to give the sanction of his sacred name to the most odious measures, and to the most unjustifiable public declarations from a throne ever renowned for truth, honour and unsullied virtue.

THE HONOUR OF THE CROWN

Wilkes went on to detail his disgust at the terms of the peace and the methods used to secure its ratification. He proceeded to consider the measures which had been proposed to substantiate the peace and to convert the national economy to a peace-time orientation, and developed his argument against what he saw as the arbitrary powers which were being relied on to get these proposals through:

A despotic minister will always endeavour to dazzle his prince with high flown ideas of the prerogative and honour of the Crown, which the minister will make a parade of firmly maintaining. I wish as much as any man in the kingdom to see the honour of the Crown maintained in a manner truly becoming Royalty. I lament to see it sunk even to prostitution. What a shame was it to see the security of this country, in point of military force, complimented away, contrary to the opinion of Royalty itself, and sacrificed to the prejudices and to the ignorance of a set of people, the most unfit from every consideration to be consulted on a matter relative to the security of the house of Hanover!

Wilkes then gave irrevocable form to the opinion of Pitt and Temple and many others that the influence of John Stuart, Earl of Bute had not been eradicated from the government by his formal resignation, but still lingered

75

in policy decided behind the curtains of the King's private chambers. He characterised the surviving ministers as 'the tools of despotism and corruption' and warned, 'They have sent the spirit of discord through the land and I will prophesy it will never be extinguished but by the extinction of their power.' And he wove into his argument the classic Whig doctrine, forged in the fire of seventy years of confrontation with the Stuart kings, that 'the King of England is only the first magistrate of this country . . . responsible to his people for the due exercise of his royal functions.'

The Stuart line has ever been intoxicated with the slavish doctrines of the *absolute, independent, unlimited* power of the Crown. Some of that line were so weakly advised as to endeavour to reduce them into practice: but the English nation was too spirited to suffer the least encroachment on the ancient liberties of this kingdom. The King of England is only the first magistrate of this country; but is invested by law with the whole of the executive power. He is, however, responsible to his people for the due exercise of the royal functions, in the choice of ministers, etc. equally with the meanest of his subjects in his particular duty.

The personal character of our present amiable sovereign makes us easy and happy that so great a power is lodged in such hands; but the *favourite* has given too just cause for him to escape the general odium. The prerogative of the Crown is to exert the constitutional powers entrusted to it in a way, not of blind favour and partiality, but of wisdom and judgment. This is the spirit of our constitution. The people too have their prerogative, and, I hope, the fine words of Dryden will be engraven on our hearts, 'Freedom is the English subject's Prerogative.'

PREROGATIVE . . . the sovereign right which has no restriction, is no longer the emotive and allusive word which stirred hearts, by-passed logic, and could be abused to justify violence. It was a word which a demagogue might conjure with in the eighteenth century, but Wilkes himself had not overplayed its influence. He had used it reasonably and with dignity. Grave men hoped that the King and his Government would recognise this.

INTOLERABLE OPPOSITION

The King and the government, however, interpreted the attack as a dangerous continuation of intolerable opposition. The resignation of Bute had not scotched the snake – now they were determined to kill it. *The North Briton's* manifesto was, as usual, unsigned, and they therefore decided to proceed by the method of the general warrant. While Wilkes busied himself with preparing the next issue of his paper, they took legal opinion, and were assured of the validity of the weapon of the general

The North Briton, *No. 45, becomes symbolic.*
NATIONAL PORTRAIT GALLERY

warrant. After an appreciable delay, they ordered the arrest of the authors, printers and publishers of the 'seditious libel' contained in No. 45 of *The North Briton*, and further ordered the four marshals to whom the warrant was addressed to discover and remove the private papers of all those taken into custody.

The agents of the government made dawn arrests of some 48 people – many of them entirely innocent – whom they considered as likely to have been involved in the publication. They included the printers, compositors and journeyman printers attached to the partnership of Balfe and Kearsley, who had produced *The North Briton*, and the government, by arresting them, effectively prevented the issue of No. 46. Interrogation of the printers gave the authorities ground for assuming that Wilkes was the author. On the night of Friday 29 April, two government bailiffs warily positioned themselves outside Wilkes's house in Great George Street, at the Whitehall end of Birdcage Walk. But when Wilkes came home at midnight, they refrained from arresting him. Afterwards they justified this inaction by saying that Wilkes was 'in liquor'.

Wilkes went out early next morning, airily observing to the government runners that he would be back for breakfast, and again they let him pass. He walked to the office of his printers, in the Strand, where he broke in and

Playing for time – and habeas corpus.
MANSELL COLLECTION

78

Lord Halifax. 'We have not been introduced,' said Wilkes.

'pied' the type already set for the printing of No. 46. He destroyed other papers which he thought might be incriminating, and strolled back home.

I SHALL RUN YOU THROUGH

The officers in Great George Street at last plucked up their courage to take him. They showed him the general warrant, and added that they had verbal orders from Lord Egremont, one of the Secretaries of State, to arrest him under the warrant. Wilkes refused to recognise these orders and said the officers might, with equal justification, arrest Egremont himself under the general warrant. 'Why do you serve it on me?' he asked. 'Why not rather serve it on the Lord Chancellor, or either of the Secretaries?' His squint-eyes twinkled as he suggested: 'Why not serve it on Lord Bute – or my next-door neighbour?'

Wilkes was enjoying himself, but he was also playing for time. It was still early in the morning, and he could not rely on any of his friends being yet out of bed and active. The bailiffs were as bovine as could be expected of their calling, indeed a little thicker-witted than the average of their

'Good morning, Mr. Thompson,' said Wilkes with a leer to Churchill, giving his aide the tip to flee from London.
NATIONAL PORTRAIT GALLERY

fellows, for the most intelligent of the government runners had anticipated trouble in the dubious execution of the controversial general warrant, and had sent in a false certificate saying he was too sick to work. By this means he saved himself from being sued later in a number of successful actions for damages. The officers in Great George Street shuffled uneasily as Wilkes made verbal mincemeat of them, and one of them impatiently put out his hand to take Wilkes by the shoulder. The Member of Parliament half-drew his sword. 'Touch me, and I shall run you through,' he promised.

Eventually the officers were persuaded to go inside Wilkes's house and continue the argument there. Wilkes's friends began to arrive, and two of them swiftly left to procure a writ of habeas corpus. Charles Churchill, Wilkes's assistant in the production of *The North Briton*, unexpectedly called. He was one of the 'authors' whom the bailiffs had been ordered to bring in, but they did not recognise him. Before Churchill could make any remark that might disclose his identity, Wilkes greeted him effusively. '*Mr Thomson!*' he said. 'Good morrow, *Mr Thomson*. How does Mrs Thomson do today? Does she dine *in the country*?' Churchill immediately understood the situation, left the house hurriedly, and sped home to collect any incriminating papers and take refuge outside London.

Lord Halifax, one of the Secretaries of State, was fully aware of the obstructive tactics being practised at Wilkes's house, since he himself lived in Great George Street only a few doors away. He sent a messenger asking Wilkes to visit him there. Wilkes formally declined, saying that he had not previously had the honour of being introduced to Halifax and therefore it was not done in polite society that he should call on him. Finally a squad of government officers arrived at Wilkes's house with instructions to cut the cackle and nab the man. Wilkes, who saw himself as another Hampden, demanded their removal, assuring them, 'I know and shall support the rights of an Englishman in his own house.' The officer in charge of the party swore to Wilkes that he would call out a platoon of the Guards to

The Earl of Egremont, son of a Jacobite once imprisoned in Wilkes's cell in the Tower of London.
NATIONAL PORTRAIT GALLERY

take him by force if necessary. At about noon, therefore, Wilkes, having made all his polemical points from Magna Carta onwards, consented to go to Halifax's house, but declined to walk under the rough escort that was now thronging the precincts. He instructed the bailiffs to order a sedan-chair, and was carried the few steps to Halifax's door.

Halifax had prepared, in a big room overlooking St James's Park, a sort of Chamber of the Inquisition manned by himself and Egremont as Secretaries of State, with the Law Officers of the Crown and a gaggle of under-secretaries. Wilkes refused to submit to any interrogation. Instead, he made a spirited speech assuring the *ad hoc* court that at the earliest moment he would raise the matter of his illegal arrest before the House of Commons. After further abortive questioning and long periods of silence, there was a commotion outside as two Members of Parliament supporting Wilkes brought the writ of habeas corpus which had now been granted. Halifax was by now more than uneasy at the news that the Lord Chief Justice of the Court of Common Pleas had by this action declared, at the least pending further consideration, against general warrants. As many men do when they are rattled during the midst of arbitrary actions, Halifax hastily plunged farther into the quicksands of peremptory power, virtually committing the authority of the establishment to rescue him if necessary, rather than retreat towards rationality and compromise.

Halifax asked Wilkes where he preferred to be imprisoned – in his own house, in Newgate Gaol or in the Tower of London. Wilkes replied that he did not take favours from any but those whom he already listed among his friends, and the choice was academic since a writ of habeas corpus had already been granted. Halifax said he was taking the advice of the Treasury Solicitor that the writ no longer applied. It had been addressed by name to the two government officers who had originally accosted Wilkes, but they had now handed Wilkes over to the Secretaries of State, and since they no longer held him they could not release him; the Secretaries of State possessed the power of committal granted to magistrates, and Halifax was despatching Wilkes to the Tower.

FEAR OF THE POX

Wilkes was transferred to the Tower of London, where he was put in close confinement. He made an elaborate play of seeking assurance that his cell was not that in which any Scotsman had previously been confined, 'for fear of the pox'. As a last resort, he said, he would accept the dungeon

*Frederick, Prince of Wales, the son of
George II. He died in 1715 and the
succession thus passed directly to George
II's grandson.*

'The King Who Lost America': George
III (1738–1820). A formal, and
flattering, contemporary portrait.

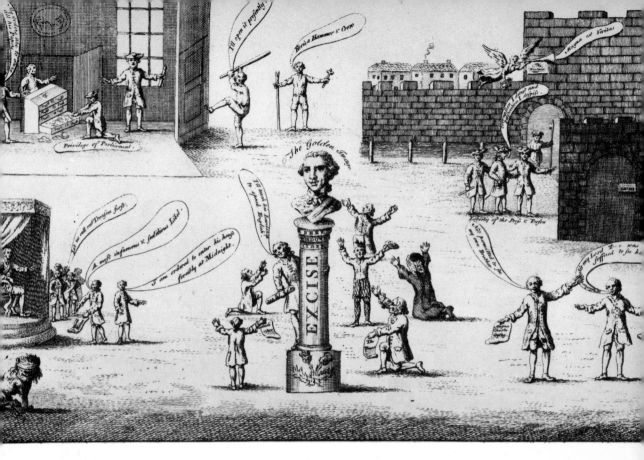

Cartoon tribute to Wilkes after his arrest.

that had been occupied by Sir William Wyndham. His point was that Wyndham, the father of Lord Egremont, one of the Secretaries who had committed him, had been imprisoned in the Tower as a Jacobite, but as an English Tory Jacobite, not a Scot. A ballad-maker swiftly exploited the incident:

> *When Scottish Oppression reared up its damned head,*
> *And old English Liberty almost was dead,*
> *Brave Wilkes, like a true English Member, arose,*
> *And thundered Defiance against England's foes.*
> > *O sweet Liberty! Wilkes and Liberty!*
> > *Old English Liberty, O!*
>
> *To daunt him in vain with Confinement they tried,*
> *But ah his great soul e'en the Tower defied.*
> *'Conduct me kind Sir' (to the Jailer he said)*
> *'Where never Scotch Rebel nor Traitor was laid.'*

But the Jailer knew well it was not in his power
To find such a place anywhere in the Tower,
So begged, if he could, he'd the Lodging think well on,
Although it smelt strongly of Scotch and Rebellion.
   O sweet Liberty! Wilkes and Liberty!
   Old English Liberty, O!

Immediately Wilkes had been taken from Great George Street the government lawyers and bailiffs moved into his house and ransacked it for papers, breaking open his desks and drawers and carting away in sacks everything they found. In order to secure the legal cover of the presence of a 'prisoner's friend', the Treasury Solicitor asked Lord Temple if he would witness the seizure of the papers. But Temple fiercely refused to take part in an action 'too barbarous for any human eye'. No doubt the indignation was exaggerated for political publicity, but there is no doubt that, in the eyes of contemporary observers, the violent despoiling and confiscation of private papers, not only with regard to Wilkes but to the other 48 prisoners in humbler circumstances, appeared to be a scandalous trespass on freedom. Today it is more equably accepted as part of the apparatus of state security, possibly because the locks are broken more privately without the cautious invitation of defence representatives to witness the intrusion. The forms of liberty were more scrupulously regarded in the past.

KING GEORGE'S VENDETTA

King George III had taken an intense personal participation in the action against Wilkes. Many modern historians mask this vendetta aspect, saying that the Ministry made all the decisions and George constitutionally abided by them. But it was the King who eagerly perused the reports of the interrogation of the printers and the others arrested earlier. It was the King who sent word to Halifax, while he was still confronting Wilkes in the afternoon of April 30, that the interrogations showed that Wilkes and Churchill were the only writers responsible for *The North Briton*, and that the original copy for No. 45 had been in the handwriting of Wilkes alone. It was the King who, once Wilkes was incarcerated in the Tower, sent word to the Lord Lieutenant of Buckinghamshire that Wilkes was immediately to be dismissed from his position as Colonel of the Buckinghamshire Militia – a personal act of vengeance which affected Wilkes more

The Ways of Man are before the Eyes of the LORD And

Fear God. — Honour the King. — and Rejoice —

Mark IV.22 — King George the Third was 22 Years of Age the 4th of June 1760 — His most Excellent Majesty

Deduced from — The Infallible Word of Truth — The Divine Oracles.

Royal Declarations. PROVERBS, Chap. XIX y14 Chap. XXXI. V.10.
Verse14 A Prudent Wife is from the Lord 10. Her Price is far above Rubies.

Chap. III. v. 6.7

V. 6th In all thy ways acknowledge GOD, and He shall direct thy Paths.7 Be not wise in thine own Eyes. Fear the Lord.

PSALM. The XXXVII. V. 4.34.

V. 4th Delight thy self also in the Lord and He shall give thee the desires of thine Heart v.34 Wait on the Lord

PROVERBS, Chap. XVI. v. 3.6.

V. 3th Commit thy Works unto the Lord and thy thoughts shall be established v.6 By the fear of the Lord Men depart from Evil

V. 12th It is an Abomination to Kings to commit Wickedness for the Throne is established by Righteousness.

Chap. XXIV. v. 5.6.

V. 5th A Wise Man is strong, yea a Man of knowledge increaseth strength

V. 6th For by wise Counsel thou shalt make thy War and in Multitude of Counsellors there is safety.

George III, a pious young man who
forced his Ministers to prayer meetings
in the draughty corridors of Windsor
Castle.

87

keenly than many of his subsequent deprivations; for he had done the state some service by military duty during the wartime scare of a French invasion, and he was extremely proud of his rank and the red coat which he had frequently worn to mark it. The Lord Lieutenant of Buckinghamshire was Lord Temple, who wrote a letter accepting his instructions but regretting 'the loss of an officer, by his deportment in command, endeared to the whole corps'. For this insubordination King George dismissed Lord Temple as his Lord Lieutenant. The post was immediately applied for, and granted to, Sir Francis Dashwood, recently dismissed as Chancellor of the Exchequer after what is considered the most disastrous year the Treasury ever knew, but raised to the Lords and sitting as Baron Le Despenser, a 'King's Friend'.

Temple meanwhile had applied to the Chief Justice of the Court of Common Pleas for a new writ of habeas corpus and an examination of the subterfuge by which the former writ had been evaded. (The Chief Justice of the King's Bench, where the case might also have been heard, was considered too ardent a King's Friend.) At an interim hearing three days after Wilkes's arrest the Court immediately ordered a relaxation of Wilkes's close confinement in the Tower, and permitted him to receive visitors. But the King, in his last reference to Wilkes by his military rank, ordered the Governor of the Tower to keep a list of the names of 'all who applied for admission to Colonel Wilkes', and this order was shown as sardonic intimidation to every visitor.

PEOPLE MOST IN NEED OF PROTECTION

At the interim hearing of the Court of Common Pleas where Sir Charles Pratt (later Lord Chancellor Camden), the Chief Justice, was deciding on the habeus corpus appeal, Wilkes spoke directly to the huge gallery in and beyond the court when he declared, 'I trust that the consequences of this hearing will teach ministers of arbitrary principles that the liberty of an English subject is not to be sported away with impunity in this cruel and despotic manner'. At the final hearing, three days later, Pratt did not hand down a binding judgment on the legality of general warrants.* But he was unhesitating about his decision on the personal liberty of Wilkes. Wilkes, in a preliminary speech at this hearing, had said in words which were to become increasingly significant of his political attitude as twenty further years of struggle passed, 'The liberty of all peers and gentlemen, and, what touches me more sensibly, that of the middling and inferior set of people, who stand most in need of protection, is in my case this day to be finally decided on: a question of such importance as to determine at once whether English liberty shall be a reality or a shadow.' Pratt did not in fact declare for 'the middling and inferior set of people'. But he gave judgment that Wilkes, as a Member of Parliament, ought not to have been arrested for libel and must be immediately released.

---

* Seven months later, in his summing up of an action from which Wilkes got £1000 for wrongful arrest, Pratt declared, 'This warrant is unconstitutional, illegal and absolutely void.' A few weeks afterwards, the House of Commons debated a declaratory motion condemning general warrants as illegal, but the Government put on extraordinary pressure to whip in support to reject it, and the motion was narrowly defeated. That decision had no force in law, and would not have had if the motion had been carried. But the Wilkes case and the resulting public outcry resulted in a realisation by Authority that the general warrant was no longer a conveniently acceptable instrument of state repression. Today both *general warrants* (ordering the arrest of unnamed persons without previous evidence of their guilt or knowledge of their identities) and *general search warrants* (empowering messengers to seize documents with similar disregard to previous evidence) are flatly illegal.

Lord Halifax was sued by Wilkes for damages – but kept him waiting for the money.
MARY EVANS COLLECTION

Lord Sandwich was booed at the Beggar's Opera.
MARY EVANS COLLECTION

WILKES AND LIBERTY!

The sequel was an immediate uproar of popular approval, primed from the public benches inside the courtroom and taken up with frenzied cheering from the large crowd outside. Wilkes was lifted on to sweaty shoulders and chaired into the street, where for the first time there was heard the cry that was to become the rallying call for many years of opposition to King George III, 'Wilkes and Liberty!'

At any assessment it was a more philosophical, and certainly more gratifying, slogan than Wilkes's previous mottoes, whether they were '*Fay ce que vouldras*' or 'Beef and Liberty!' The truth was that any further association with Dashwood at Medmenham or at the Beefsteak Club with Lord Sandwich in the chair was doomed. Sandwich, another old fellow-roisterer from the fraternity of St Francis at Medmenham, was to replace Egremont as Secretary of State, and to pay for the King's favour by becoming the chief engineer in plotting the downfall of Wilkes. So potent and public a renegade did he become that he was swiftly known popularly as Jemmy Twitcher, after the plaintive recrimination of Macheath, the highwayman in *The Beggar's Opera*, 'That Jemmy Twitcher should peach, I own surprised me. 'Tis a proof that the world is all alike, and that even our gang can no more trust one another than other people.' Sandwich was drummed out of the Sublime Society of Beefsteaks.

The government was determined to destroy Wilkes, as Lord Halifax personally assured him. Immediately after his release by Pratt, and his confirmation that his private papers were missing, Wilkes wrote to the Secretaries of State accusing them as receivers of stolen property, 'I find that my house has been robbed and am informed that the stolen goods are in the possession of one or both of your lordships. I therefore insist that you do forthwith return them to your humble servant.' Halifax replied that Wilkes was to be prosecuted by the Attorney General and his papers would be kept until it had been decided which were proofs of his guilt.

Wilkes was delighted to keep the agitation going. He not only sued Halifax and his under-secretary for damages, but persuaded all the 48 others who had been arrested under the general warrant to do the same. The London juries, who in general had no parliamentary franchise, voted with their verdicts, and as a result thousands of pounds were secured for printers and compositors.

CRITICISM SUPPRESSED

Politically, the King could be pardoned if he considered that he had gained certain immediate fruits of victory. He had at least extinguished *The North Briton*. By doing so, he had certainly saved himself from con-

Egremont was fired as Secretary of State.
MARY EVANS COLLECTION

Hogarth produced his most offensive
portrait of the squinting Wilkes.
MARY EVANS COLLECTION

siderable public harassment through the summer of 1763. He possessed a fragment of issue No. 46, which would have been published on the day of Wilkes's arrest if he had not been struck with the general warrant. This, though still maintaining a front of loyalty, attacked the King in personal terms for the policies of both past and future. Wilkes had taken as his topic the National Day of Prayer and Thanksgiving which the King had ordained for Thursday 5 May in celebration of the Peace. 'Religion,' stormed Wilkes,

is now made a political state-engine to serve the vilest and most infamous purposes of an abandoned minister or of a wicked and corrupt administration . . . prostituted to the shameful ends of faction and party. I am led into these reflections by the form of prayer and thanksgiving to Almighty God, for putting an end to the late bloody and expensive war, by the conclusion of a just and honourable peace.

It is notable that, once the King had dismissed Pitt, he had selected, in his description of the Seven Years War, the precise terms 'bloody and expensive' which Pitt had struck out of the published version of the King's Speech over two years previously.

I look upon this to be a most daring insult on the common sense of mankind, and not only an outrage to the public, but a solemn mockery of the Divine Being. Are we by a ministerial mandate to thank God that the Scot has sacrificed our most important conquests to the inveterate enemies of our religion and liberties?

THE THREAT

Wilkes analysed in detail his view of the injustices of the peace treaty. He counselled the King not to go to St Paul's Cathedral and, for the first time, gave indirect incitement to the London mob to intervene if such a State procession were mounted. The King might justifiably give his own 'Thank God' that such sedition had not been published:

I always feel the truest rapture when I see the most excellent prince in Europe, the delight of his people, appearing in public to subjects who build their own happiness on that of their amiable monarch. Yet I own, I hope my sovereign will not go on Thursday in solemn procession to St Paul's, because I fear the censure of the malicious and ill-intentioned. I believe the city of London, so justly renowned for the high spirit of liberty, tempered with the firmest loyalty to their princes, was not gratified with the presence of their beloved King, either after the taking of Martinique, Pondicherry or the Havannah.

  If gratitude to heaven in all these great events was shewn by our pious prince rather in private devotion than in any solemn public act, I should hope (if I may be allowed to form a wish on this great occasion, that the humiliating circumstance of giving up so many and important conquests was not to be attended with parade or ostentation; for, I confess, *I fear the ill-humour which is too visible in the body of the people*, and the late attack on their liberties by enlarging the dominion of that accursed fiend, the Excise. I hope, therefore, that on the day of thanksgiving for the Peace, his Majesty will only go to the chapel, and that all bloody swords being now sheathed and laid aside, the peaceful wooden sword of state will be carried by that excellent peace officer, Lord George Sackville.

I AM MY OWN MAN

The envenomed shaft of the last phrase, which forcefully burst the bubble of any pious pretensions of loyalty in the preceding passage, was directed against a routine butt, the 47-year-old son of the Duke of Dorset. Commanding the British forces in the Battle of Minden, 1759, Lord George Sackville failed to execute the orders of his commander-in-chief to charge at a critical moment, and the impact of the victory was impaired. A court martial, virulently encouraged by George II, adjudged him incapable of serving henceforth in any military capacity. But on the accession of George III Sackville returned to public life. As Secretary of State for the Colonies after 1775 he was to have the virtual direction of the disastrous British military role in the War of American Independence. Wilkes had already written for private circulation a reference to him as engaged in homosexual relations with the Primate of Ireland – which was to provide part of the evidence for the impending public downfall of the Member for Aylesbury.

Throughout the summer of 1763 the tumult for Wilkes and Liberty was kept continuously alive as the verdicts awarding damages to the printers of *The North Briton* were announced in sequence. The King had won a political battle, but the struggle seemed to have been consigned to the warfare of the streets. However, the government agents had been strongly deployed to prepare an autumn offensive. Wilkes had spies at his door, suborners at his servants' entrance, and secret examiners of his mail. He was rash and ingenious enough to present all of them with ammunition. 'I hear from all hands that the King is enraged at my insolence, as he terms it,' Wilkes wrote to Temple – and the King duly read it in copy. 'I will ever be his faithful subject, not his servant. Hypocrisy, meanness, ignorance and insolence characterise the King I obey. My independent spirit will never take a favour from such a man. I am my own man, and Lord Temple's.'

RISKY VENTURE

But Wilkes was not notably subservient to Lord Temple, except when he solicited one of his frequent loans from his patron. He was anxious to reprint all published copies of *The North Briton* and, finding no printer who was willing to take the risk, installed a press in his Great George Street house, entirely contrary to Temple's advice. On this press he ran off the 45 numbers of his paper, which brought him renewed renown and a considerable financial loss. It also, by repeating publication of matter over which a prosecution had been promised, ran his head halfway into the noose which the King was holding open for him. The rest of the action which achieved his painful suspense was provided by skilful government knavery. Before the publication of No. 45 Wilkes had used the press of his printer to run off the first pages of a long pornographic poem entitled *An Essay on Woman*. A reference to this work had been secured when Wilkes's papers were commandeered at the time of his arrest. Wilkes was aware of this and, in some bravado, he promptly published a newspaper advertisement announcing the imminent publication of *An Essay on Woman* by the Treasury Solicitor.

The government spent many weeks of effort to secure a printed version

*Minden, where Lord George Sackville
failed to charge at a critical moment.*
MARY EVANS COLLECTION

of this damaging composition. Eventually government spies managed to bribe a dissident printer who had been discharged by Wilkes after attempting blackmail, and they were in possession of a proof-copy of the bawdy work. It had not been intended for publication, but only for private circulation among Wilkes's friends, probably the monks at Medmenham. The government later accounted for their possession of this evidence by a tale that the printer had rested his pot of beer one lunch-time on a discarded page and had been so appalled by what he read that he had secured the full set of the first pages printed. There is strong evidence that, having secured the exhibit, government agents forged emendations to make it more repulsive. When one reads the copy, this seems hardly to have been necessary, except in the instance of one blatant passage which the King could have taken as a depraved personal reference.

Wilkes went to Paris to supervise the education of his daughter Polly, and other self-indulgences. Having all the evidence they needed, the King and his principal ministers – and there is no doubt that they worked in close collusion – settled down to prepare in the finest detail an assault on Wilkes timed for the opening of Parliament on 15 November 1763. They finalised for the House of Commons a charge against Wilkes, for which he was fully prepared, of publishing and re-publishing the 'seditious libel' in *The North Briton*. They had an indictment before the House of Lords, of which he was completely ignorant, of printing a 'scandalous, impious and obscene libel' against a member of that House in *An Essay on Woman*. By skilful parliamentary engineering they exploded both mines before Wilkes could take the slightest cover.

A MESSAGE FROM THE KING

The agent somewhat craftily chosen by King George III to fuse this petard was George Grenville, the stop-gap Prime Minister whom the King had appointed to succeed Bute with the sole intention (as the King assured Bute) of securing independent action for himself, George III. Grenville had been Wilkes's second patron and prompter in the earlier issues of *The North Briton*, and had indeed unwittingly provided the subject matter for No. 45. But now he was remote in his function as first minister of the King.

Wilkes stood up at the start of business in the new session of the Commons to raise the question of breach of privilege in connection with his arrest under the general warrant. His purpose was known, and normally

*Lord North served his apprenticeship as
the King's man against America by
acting as the King's man against Wilkes.*
MARY EVANS COLLECTION

a matter of privilege had absolute priority in the House. But Grenville rose
immediately and announced: 'Mr Speaker, Sir. I have a message from His
Majesty the King.'

The Speaker, who had been in private conference with Grenville, said
that he would take the King's message first. Pitt rose in protest and argued
at dramatic length that nothing should take precedence over the privileges

of Members. A heated debate ensued, but when the vote was taken the Speaker was supported in his ruling. Grenville delivered the message from the King:

His Majesty having received information that John Wilkes Esquire, a Member of this House, was the author of a most dangerous and seditious libel ... apprehended but discharged by the Court of Common Pleas on ground of privilege ... ignored a summons to appear before the King's Bench ... His Majesty deeming it of the utmost importance not to suffer the public justice of this Kingdom to be eluded ... laid the libel before his faithful Commons for their consideration.

INCITING INSURRECTION

Lord North then rose for the Government to propose a motion that No. 45 of *The North Briton* was a false, scandalous and seditious libel containing expressions of the most unexampled insolence and contumely towards His Majesty, the grossest aspersions on both Houses of Parliament and the most audacious defiance of the authority of the whole Legislature, most manifestly tending to alienate the affections of the people from His Majesty, to withdraw them from their obedience to the Laws of the Realm, and to excite them to traitorous insurrection against His Majesty's Government.

Wilkes had to settle down to an evening of abuse and, as it resulted, an attempt on his life. Outstanding among his attackers was the Government's expert at corruption, Samuel Martin, Secretary of the Treasury. *The North Briton* had described him (*but not in No. 45*, which made his remarks irrelevant to the debate) as treacherous, lowlived and dirty among a number of other adjectives. Martin reminded the House of this editorial disapproval, and said, 'A man capable of writing in that manner without putting his name to it, and thereby stabbing another man in the dark, is a cowardly, malignant and scandalous scoundrel. A cowardly rascal, a malignant villain, and an infamous scoundrel.' Wilkes realised that he had a duel on his hands in the morning.

SANCTIMONIOUS HORROR

Meanwhile in the House of Lords the Earl of Sandwich was on his feet with a complaint that John Wilkes, a member of the lower house, had libelled a member of the House of Lords, William Warburton, Lord Bishop of Gloucester. To 'prove' the libel he then read aloud with the greatest relish, but with many exclamations of shock and horror, the whole of the printed section available to the government of the text and footnotes of the pornographic *An Essay on Woman*. At times there were cries of protest that this quotation *in extenso* should cease. But the majority of the Lords were enjoying not only the scurrilous text which Wilkes had printed, but the sanctimonious horror interpolated by the comments of Sandwich, whose reputation for public obscenity was second to none. They roared appreciatively that the recital should continue, and it did. The Bishop of Gloucester, who had been shamefully parodied in the skit, *which was now being published for the first time by Sandwich, and quite unnecessarily*, rose in almost inarticulate fury to declare, also unnecessarily, that he had not written a line of this filth. The poem was solemnly ratified, by vote of the Lords, as a most scandalous, obscene and impious libel, and there was no doubt that Wilkes would be prosecuted before the King's Bench for having printed it.

The government had deliberately introduced the matter of *An Essay on Woman* as a second barrel to get Wilkes condemned by public opinion on moral grounds if they could not secure his condemnation for alleged sedition. King George III had the utmost justification for being revolted by it, but no equitable excuse for prosecuting Wilkes for printing it, since

Bishop Warburton, a first-time father at 57, was sensitive about any witticism involving Potter.

there had never been any intention to publish. The mainly dissolute ministers who joined the conspiracy to ruin Wilkes had neither aesthetic nor juridical extenuation for their action.

An Essay on Woman had, in fact, been written by Wilkes's crony, Thomas Potter, who had died in 1759, and much of it was eighteen years old, dating from about 1745, when Wilkes was a student at Leyden and had not yet met Potter. Wilkes had, however, revised one or two passages to make the allusions topical, and he had certainly written some of the footnotes, which were attributed to the Bishop of Gloucester. These footnotes were ultra-pedantic comments which were intended to be humorous because of the incongruity of their learned style with their bawdy matter. The pretence that they had been written by William Warburton, Bishop of Gloucester, was a literary joke which Gloucester might well have had the courage to accept – for Warburton had applied precisely the same 'scholarly' humour to his published notes in official editions of Pope's satiric poem *The Dunciad*, when his butt had been a failed poet named Bentley. But Warburton had a more delicate reason for revenge against the dead Potter, and anyone associated with a revision of his work. When Warburton was 57, and childless after a dozen years of marriage, his wife became acquainted with Potter. Almost immediately she became pregnant. The child was born, and while Society congratulated Warburton, it turned aside to smirk. The Bishop was therefore understandably sensitive. The reading of bawdy comments attributed to him in the presence of peers purple-faced with hilarity was undoubtedly hurtful, but the ascription of these indecent comments to him would have been more clearly libellous if the poem had ever been truly published, rather than having been stolen from Wilkes's desk and assiduously reprinted by the House of Lords as 'evidence'.

REMORSELESSLY BORING

The contemporary impact of *An Essay on Woman* was that it was a line-by-line parody of Pope's *An Essay on Man*, a pseudo-philosophic work which at that time was known almost by heart to every man of education. (Pope had frankly admitted in his introduction to the essay that he could have written it in prose. 'But I chose verse, and even rhyme, for two reasons . . . That principles, maxims, or precepts so written both strike the reader more strongly at first and are more easily retained by him afterwards . . . and I found I could express them more *shortly* this way than in prose itself.') Potter had merely re-written the work as a parody with an entirely phallic impact. *An Essay on Man* is jejune and boring to the modern reader because of the meagre and scanty profundity of its text and of the would-be scholarly commentary by Warburton. *An Essay on Woman* is even more boring today because of the immature insistence on the penis, or pego as the current cant word for it was then. The only technical interest is the remorseless ingenuity with which, line by line, Potter and Wilkes converted every high-flown sentiment and simile of Pope into a reference to the mechanics of intercourse.

The original title-page of Pope's work ran: *An Essay on Man* BY Alexander Pope Esq WITH THE NOTES OF William, Lord Bishop of Gloucester. It was followed by an engraved medallion showing the head of Pope. The title-page of the parody read: *An Essay on Woman*, BY Pego Borewell Esq WITH NOTES BY Rogerus Cunaeus, Vigerus Mutoniatus, AND A COMMENTARY BY The Rev Dr Warburton. INSCRIBED TO Miss Fanny Murray. (Fanny Murray was a notable prostitute of the 1740s, of whom it was said that she was once so disgusted with receiving only a £20 note for her services that she put the banknote between two slices of bread and ate it as a sandwich.) There followed, not a medallion of the author, but the engraving of a phallus, below which was a note in Latin which read, in translation: FROM THE ORIGINAL FREQUENTLY IN THE CRUTCH OF THE Most Reverend George Stone, Primate of Ireland, MORE FREQUENTLY IN THE ANUS OF THE INTREPID HERO George Sackville.

SENSITIVE KING

The scurrilous imputation on Lord George Sackville, whom George III had restored to favour after George II had disgraced him for his conduct at the battle of Minden, cannot have endeared the parody to the reigning monarch even from its very first page. The coarseness of the text that

Bishop Warburton, 'I never wrote a line of this filth!'
NATIONAL PORTRAIT GALLERY

followed must have been insupportable. George III was eminently shockable, not having had the benefit of a contemporary university education or a lordly training in profligacy. But even the least squeamish of men can be revolted by the inclusion in a composition consistently bawdy of a reference to the sexual capacity or dimensions of his mother. King George, already hyper-sensitive concerning the gossip about his mother and Lord Bute, must have been understandably seared to the heart by a gratuitously offensive passage which – it was long presumed by him – Wilkes himself inserted.

The original of this passage ran in Pope's original, as he philosophised about Man's precedence and rank in the hierarchy of the created Universe:

> Ask of thy mother Earth, why oaks are made
> Taller or stronger than the weeds they shade?
> Or ask of yonder argent fields above
> Why Jove's satellites are less than Jove?
> Of Systems possible, if 'tis confest
> That Wisdom infinite must form the best,
> Where all must full or not coherent be,
> And all that rises, rise in due degrees;
> Then, in the scale of reas'ning life, 'tis plain
> There must be, somewhere, such a rank as Man.

This rather plodding logic was parodied in *An Essay on Woman* into:

> Ask of thy Mother's Cunt why she was made
> Of lesser bore than Cow or hackney'd Jade?
> Or ask thy raw-bon'd Scottish Father's Tarse
> Why larger he than Stallion or Jack-Ass?
> Of Pego's possible, if 'tis confess'd
> That Wisdom infinite must form some best,
> Where all must rise, or not coherent be,
> And all that rise must rise in due degree,
> Then in the scale of various Pricks, 'tis plain
> Godlike erect, BUTE stands the foremost man.

To this passage Wilkes, or another, appended a mock-scholarly footnote 'by Bishop Warburton' gravely comparing the penis of the donkey (Jack-Ass) with the organs of the rest of creation, and justifying its size.

George III: eminently shockable without a public school education.
MARY EVANS COLLECTION

FORGED EVIDENCE

The reference to Bute was generally attributed to Wilkes. There would certainly have been no topical allusion when the work was first written by Potter. But there is another possible source for it. It is known that the government forged some passages in their version of *An Essay on Woman* in order to be sure that a charge of obscene libel would stick. Wilkes himself, owing to absence from the Trial Court and the refusal of Lord Chief Justice Mansfield to allow notes of evidence to be taken, was never sure of what excerpts from the parody had been cited. He declared, however, that 'the most wretched and impious lines' in the work had been forged – and, indeed, there would be little point in forging anything but the most harmful. The verses in the passage which must have wounded King George most deeply are of no particular merit as wit, and the probability must be considered that, if this alleged effusion of Wilkes intensified the King's hatred and sharpened the vendetta against the Member for Aylesbury, it may well have been concocted by the forger who certainly operated in a falsification of evidence.

The shoddy business in the House of Lords was finished, and the grim consequence of condemnation for an obscene libel hinted to Wilkes, long before the end of the debate in the House of Commons condemning No. 45 of *The North Briton* as a seditious libel. There, the proceedings dragged on through the night, long after Samuel Martin had made his virtual challenge to a fight. In the early hours of the morning the vote was taken, and Wilkes

106

was condemned by a five-to-two majority of 162. In addition he had to bear the stigma of hearing an order that a copy of No. 45 should be burnt by the common hangman. Wilkes dully rose to raise the question of breach of parliamentary privilege which he had been baulked from introducing twelve hours previously. Nobody listened.

Wilkes's main case against the general warrant rested on the fact that he did not publicly admit authorship of *The North Briton*, and could not therefore be taken on a warrant not naming him. As a private gentleman, he scorned to take that cover. Wilkes wrote to Martin that morning, 'You complained yesterday, before five hundred gentlemen, that you had been *stabbed in the dark*; but I have reason to believe that you were not so *in the dark* as you affected to be. To cut off every pretence of ignorance as to the author, I whisper in your ear that every passage of *The North Briton* in which you have been named or even alluded to was written by Your humble servant, John Wilkes.'

A SKILFULLY MANIPULATED DUEL

Martin replied immediately in a letter which he personally delivered before going on to Hyde Park to await Wilkes for a duel. Martin's letter repeated his schoolboy insults about cowardice, and declared, 'I desire that you meet me in Hyde-park immediately with a brace of pistols each, to determine our difference.'

William Murray, Lord Chancellor Mansfield, presided over Wilkes's trial for obscenity.
MARY EVANS COLLECTION

Martin, who had had no need to stay in the Commons all night, had thus skilfully forced a duel at a moment's notice on a man who had had little sleep. Additionally, he had deprived Wilkes of his right, as the man challenged, to choose the weapons. Wilkes was an accomplished swordsman, but had been told to bring pistols. Martin had been practising pistol-shooting at a target in preparation for this duel over the eight months which he had allowed to elapse between the objectionable reference to him in *The North Briton* and the day on which he theatrically saw his honour besmirched and peremptorily called Wilkes out. It was also true that Martin, the Ministry's indispensable bribery-distributor and an office-holder in the household of the King's mother, was, as Wilkes said of Lord Talbot, 'fighting with the King's Pardon in his pocket', whereas if Wilkes killed or maimed Martin in an illegal duel he could expect no mercy.

The two men faced each other in the park, and fired. Both missed. At the second attempt the pistol Wilkes was handling, which had been prepared and passed to him by Martin, did not fire. Martin's shot hit Wilkes in the groin and he fell in great pain, telling Martin to disappear from the scene as quickly as possible and thus escape arrest if Wilkes died. Wilkes was carried to his home, where he told a servant to return Martin's incriminating letter in case Wilkes's house was searched. A surgeon was called, and subjected Wilkes to the unpleasant remedial treatment then practised. Wilkes progressed into a high fever and was in a dangerous condition for many days.

On the day of the duel, King George III, who was not unaware of Martin's action, pressed his Prime Minister, Grenville, to dismiss from his positions at Court and in the Army General Harry Conway, who had had the temerity to vote against the House of Commons motion condemning Wilkes. While Wilkes lay semi-conscious during his long fever the House of Commons proceeded into a number of debates on the related matters of parliamentary privilege, liberty of the subject and of the press, and the legality of general warrants. The King busily scribbled urgent notes to Grenville demanding interim reports on the discussions, and identification of the members principally opposing the government's line. The London mob was well aware of the significance of the debates, and put on a number of demonstrations to emphasise their battle-cry, 'Wilkes and Liberty!' The key motion, concerning the parliamentary privilege of members in cases of seditious libel, was debated on 23–24 November 1763, and the King was restless with impatience to know its progress, sending fidgety reminders

Martin scores on Wilkes after target-
practice with pistols all summer.
MARY EVANS COLLECTION

to Grenville that he must appreciate 'the great consequence of this day's debate to the very being of the Constitution'. The truth was that he had to have the motion passed in order to secure a conviction of Wilkes before the King's Bench.

The Government, calling on all its paid supporters, and those in the Chamber who looked for future advancement, was never in any danger of losing the vote, and could guarantee an almost total lack of personal support for the absent Wilkes. Even Pitt, making a dramatic appearance to orate on the sacred nature of the liberty of the subject, took care to dissociate himself from Wilkes with the thumping lie regarding 'the blasphemer of his God and libeller of his King' . . . 'I have no connection with him. I never associated or communicated with him. I know nothing of any connection with the writer of this libel.'

ROYAL PARANOIA

At four in the morning Grenville was able to report to the King that the government had won the vote by 258 to 133, but that General Conway had again voted against restricting the liberty of the subject. George now reiterated his demand for Conway's instant dismissal from the regiment which he commanded and the honorary post he held at Court, 'for in this matter I am instantly concerned. I cannot trust my Army in the hands of those that are against my measures' – an observation almost maniac in its paranoia, but a very convincing confirmation that the King regarded the government's tough line and authoritarian declarations as *his measures*.

Wilkes was extremely depressed by the renegade lie with which Pitt had abjured him. The King, in St James's, and Wilkes, in his bed in Great George Street a few hundred yards away, both waited for the next public act, the burning of No. 45 of *The North Briton* by the public executioner. The London mob, however, would not allow this. They soaked the faggots in the execution pyre, overturned the Sheriff's coach and pelted him and his strong escort once they had winkled him out of cover. The executioner could raise no fire for the symbolic burning of the paper. But the Londoners were well supplied, and ceremoniously burned· a large jackboot and a petticoat, the old symbols of Bute and Princess Augusta, amid rousing cheers for Wilkes and Temple. 'How incomprehensibly treasonable!' said the frustrated King. 'The continuance of Wilkes's impudence is amazing, when his ruin is so near.'

Instead of immediate ruin, Wilkes promptly acquired a bonus of £1000 from his suit for damages against Under-secretary Wood. (Lord Halifax, the Secretary of State, was able to defer the action against him for many years.) Over the Christmas adjournment of Parliament Wilkes went to Paris to join Polly. In the arduous journey by jolting coach and storm-tossed ship, his wound opened and he was unable to return to the House of Commons. In his absence, he was expelled from Parliament for having

General Conway: 'Dismiss him,'
ordered George III.
MARY EVANS COLLECTION

published 'Number Forty-five'. Next month he was tried, also in his absence, by Lord Chief Justice Mansfield on the King's Bench for having printed and published No. 45 and for printing *An Essay on Woman*. Mansfield entered judgment against Wilkes and issued a writ for his arrest.

The Lord Chief Justice was not only the King's friend, but a Scot – and the Scots had been roughly handled in *The North Briton*. Wilkes was convinced that it was Mansfield's intention to sentence him to life imprisonment for the two libels, and to commit him to the pillory as well. He did not return to England to surrender to immediate arrest. Accordingly England banished him, by declaring that his life was of no account, and if any Englishman cared to murder him in England there would be no prosecution. On 1 November 1764 John Wilkes was formally declared an outlaw for failure to answer a summons to appear for sentence at the Court of the King's Bench.

Outlawry and poverty kept Wilkes out of Great Britain for four years

in all, until he decided to challenge Mansfield's sentence and appeal to the English electorate. In those four years King George III nursed his hatred for John Wilkes, and began to conceive his fatal twin-antipathy for Sam Adams of Boston and the many others who shared his feelings – an attitude classically rendered as 'The King most cordially hates every American because he thinks that they have an attachment to their Liberty.' It was a very precise expression of a debilitating affliction: Royal Paranoia.

ADAMS: APPRENTICE IN AGITATION

Sam Adams was the son of a brewer, as Wilkes was the son of a distiller. He was born in Boston in 1722, being five years older than Wilkes. His father, 'Deacon' Adams, was a leader of the Congregational Church. At the age of fourteen Sam Adams was sent to Harvard College. When he graduated at the age of eighteen, he remained at Cambridge for three further years

to take his Master's degree. He went into business, but, in spite of being
financed by his father, was a conspicuous failure as a merchant, and took
refuge in the family brewery. He went into politics on a local scale, as an
activist in the Massachusetts Country Party, which resisted the autocratic
régime of the King's Governor. Like Wilkes, but a dozen years earlier, he
learned the power of the printed word, and for a short while ran an opposition newspaper. In 1756 he secured a 'civil service' post as collector of
taxes for Boston – a task of extortion at which he was remarkably in-
efficient.

From that year, political opposition was ironed out in the spirit of
national unity which pervaded the colony for the greater part of the
Seven Years War – with its serious threat to the American colonies from
the French strongpoints in Canada and in the south. Adams, who, like
Wilkes, generally combined in his campaigns an attachment to democratic

'*A View of Part of the Town in Boston in New England and British ships of war landing their Troops, 1768.*' Contemporary engraving by Paul Revere.

Sam Adams: took refuge in the family brewery.
MANSELL COLLECTION

liberty and the interests of the mercantile class, saw no advantage in harassing the government.

Once Canada was won, the Boston merchants lost a little loyalty in favour of profit, and renewed their lucrative smuggling activities. Their principal market was in the West Indian islands still held by their official enemies the French, and later the Spanish. What they were doing was perforating the Royal Navy blockade to run in the essential goods of fish, farm produce and timber that enabled the islands to hold out longer. They traded these life-giving supplies for profitable Caribbean products, notably sugar and molasses.

AGAIN THE GENERAL WARRANT

The King's Government consequently ordered a stricter enforcement of the trade and navigation laws. Regulations were, however, applied much more strictly to Massachusetts than to the other American colonies. In particular, the authorities made use of a power which had a remarkable resemblance to the general search warrant. Customs officers were granted *writs of assistance* which authorised them to enter warehouses and dwelling houses in search of contraband. The entrepreneurs in Massachusetts thought that this arbitrary measure was being used against them in a discriminatory fashion. Boston merchants combined to lead a political campaign against writs of assistance. Sam Adams saw that the grievance

*British troops escorting the stamped
paper to the city hall, New York, 1765.*
J. G. MOORE COLLECTION

could be coloured with the tints of a struggle for popular liberty, and re-commenced his interrupted career as an agitator. He had now developed as a first-rate newspaper propagandist, an eloquent demagogue, and an organiser who could manage mobs with unholy cunning.

Adams worked principally through the workingmen's clubs whose meetings were held in Boston taverns. He was always a scrupulously pious man, with the moral and religious fervour of an old Puritan. At the same time, he was a compulsive orator with an unashamed liking for good chorus singing amid a few pots of ale. He was an outstanding example of the old religio-political tub-thumper before nonconformists were swayed into teetotalism. He could have had no more appreciative audiences – and none with greater potentiality for demonstrations of mob power – than the workers and apprentices of Boston, whom he kept in political alertness and maudlin harmony with a mixture of fervent hymns and revolutionary songs.

NO REPRESENTATION

Wilkes had said he became a patriot by accident. The radical movement in both England and America not only called themselves Patriots but, curiously, were described as such by their opponents – as badly judged an exercise in public relations as the tolerance with which the right wing called themselves Tories, a name of ill-repute originally bestowed by their enemies. The Patriots were forced by circumstances to work mainly through popular propaganda and mob agitation outside the legislature, since they had virtually no representation. Boston itself sent only four members to the House of Representatives out of the Massachusetts total of 104. There was as little popular influence on the domestic government of Massachusetts as there was within the imperial Parliament in London. The upper house, known as the Council, was pretty firmly in the pocket of the Governor appointed by the King. The lower House of Representatives represented personal interest more effectively than political cause. It had a strong kernel of trusty pensioners and other members tied to the establishment by the corrupt possession or promise of lucrative office. The legislature therefore had its powerful cabal of Governor's Friends corresponding to the King's Friends in London.

The King's Friends in London were, in fact, being groomed by the increasingly crafty George III for a more sophisticated role. The King had always regarded – and unhesitatingly described – his ministers as his tools. When his ministers proved irresolute in the policy towards the American colonies, *and their irresolution was exposed to the King by the militancy of Boston under the leadership of Sam Adams*, King George intrigued against his own government. He built up his personally dependent, politically servile, Palace Guard of the King's Friends to such a strength that they, as his veritable tools, could dismiss the government on his command. The consequence was that the King assumed power, with Lord North as his mouthpiece. The consummation of that development was that the King lost America. The analysis of this sequence indicates that King George III was not then the constitutional monarch that his apologists still claim him to be, and that the crossroads point where he turned aside from constitutional monarchy can be signposted by Sam Adams's riotous direction of the Boston mob in opposition to the Stamp Act of 1765.

George Grenville, as Prime Minister after the fall of Bute, held the conventional office which signalised his precedence, First Lord of the Treasury. He regarded his Treasury duties as far more than a conventional cloak for leadership. He began a vigorous campaign for retrenchment in the national economy. He ordered slashing cuts in defence expenditure, and sought additional income to pay for the upkeep of military forces

A varied collection of worshippers and supporters for Lord North, the King's Friend.

MARY EVANS COLLECTION

retained. He turned his eye to America and determined to move against tax evasion there, and towards raising additional taxation from the colonies. He tightened the enforcement of the smuggling laws through the writs of assistance. He made the tax on molasses imported into North America theoretically more acceptable by reducing it to a realistic level but insisting on its being collected, rather than being bypassed as previously by venal Customs officials. And he announced the intention to raise fresh revenue from America – to pay for British defence expenditure on the security of the colonies – by new imposts, of which the most notorious was the Stamp Act. He proposed to levy a duty, which was already payable within Great Britain, on legal documents, commercial papers, licences and – perhaps ominously – pamphlets and newspapers.

All taxation is iniquitous to the taxed, and is expected to be. But Grenville and George III were genuinely surprised at the heat of the opposition inspired within the American colonies at the announcement that the Stamp Act had been passed.

'WHAT A BLESSING, THE STAMP ACT'

Sam Adams himself, though he had utilised the unpopularity of the measure brilliantly as a practical exercise in perfecting the tactics of opposition, was surprised by his success, though immensely gratified. For he had fought a local battle and emerged as a leader in a national campaign. 'What a blessing to us has the Stamp Act eventually proved,' he reflected. 'When the Colonies saw the common danger, they at the same time saw their mutual dependence.'

There were valid arguments that the American Colonies, which had profited enormously in financial terms from the Seven Years War, and the

Colonel Isaac Barré christened the American rebels the Sons of Liberty.
MARY EVANS COLLECTION

security which victory had brought, should now contribute to their own defence expenditure for the maintenance of their future security. But there were strong arguments on the other side, authoritatively advanced in the British House of Commons.

Colonel Isaac Barré, an Irish soldier of Huguenot descent who had served under Wolfe and was wounded at Quebec, stood in the Commons to declaim the rights of the American colonists not to be taxed without their consent.

SONS OF LIBERTY

'Children planted by your care?' he ironically asked members of Parliament. 'No! Your oppressions planted them in America. They fled from your tyranny to a then uncultivated and inhospitable country. Nourished by your indulgence? No! They grew by your neglect of them. Protected by your arms? They have nobly taken up arms in *your* defence. They are the sons of liberty.'

'The Americans are the sons, not the bastards of England,' said the elder Pitt when he came to address the House of Commons on the American opposition to taxation without representation. He strongly argued that the mother country had no right to tax communities not represented in the Parliament imposing the tax: 'They are subjects of this kingdom, equally entitled with yourselves to all the natural rights of mankind, and the peculiar privileges of Englishmen; equally bound by its laws, and equally participating in the constitution of this free country. The Americans are the sons, not the bastards of England.'

Taxation, Pitt said, could not be *imposed* by a British Government, but only *granted* by the Commons out of their own personal wealth.

Taxes are the voluntary gift and grant of the Commons alone. When in this House we give a grant, we give and grant what is our own. But, in an American tax, what do we do? We, your Majesty's Commons for Great Britain, give a grant to your Majesty of what? Of our property? No. We give a grant to your Majesty of the property of your Majesty's Commons of America. It is an absurdity in terms. The Commons of America, represented in their several Assemblies, have ever been in possession of this, their constitutional right, of giving and granting their own money. They would have been slaves if they had not enjoyed it. [Grenville] asks when were the Colonies emancipated? But I desire to know – when were they made slaves?

No slaves, but Sons of Liberty. From the time when Colonel Barré's

WILLIAM JACKSON,

an *IMPORTER*; at the *BRAZEN HEAD*,

North Side of the TOWN-HOUSE, and *Opposite the Town-Pump, in Corn-hill,* BOSTON.

It is defired that the Sons and DAUGHTERS of *LIBERTY*, would not buy any one thing of him, for in fo doing they will bring Difgrace upon *themfelves*, and their *Pofterity*, for *ever* and *ever*, AMEN

The Sons of Liberty apply a boycott to oppose the Stamp Act.

MANSELL COLLECTION

*When Lieutenant-Governor Hutchinson
gained a sympathetic feed-back from the
violence of this raid on his house Adams
fabricated the story that documents
found there showed that Hutchinson had
'invented' the Stamp Tax.*

speech was first reported in America, all the democratic clubs and societies
in the colonies re-christened themselves. Formerly they had been muffled
as mechanics' companies, fire-fighting clubs, or societies for the mutual
improvement of apprentices. Now they all became Sons of Liberty, and
their immediate objective was to defeat the Stamp Act.

TERROR TACTICS

In Boston Sam Adams already controlled the most powerful single
'underground' policy-making body – the notorious Caucus Club which has
given its name to all conspiracies of fixers and wire-pullers over the
English-speaking world. This club was already two generations old. Sam's
father, Deacon Adams, had used it to decide in advance of the Boston town
meetings all municipal appointments and local political decisions – which
were steam-rollered through the town meeting itself. By 1765 the
Caucus, led by Sam Adams and a committee of nine who strove to remain
generally anonymous (though their names are known), had enough control
to call out a mob in Boston at a day's notice.

The Stamp Act imposed a tax on documents, varying in rate between one ha'penny and one pound, which had to be paid for by the purchase of stamps from stampmasters. Sam Adams decided to terrorise the stampmasters, many of whom had snapped up the job in the hope of quick profit from commission and bribery. A mob called out by Adams and the Caucus sacked the house of Andrew Oliver, the Massachusetts Bay stampmaster who was the brother-in-law of Thomas Hutchinson, Lieutenant Governor of Massachusetts. A trembling Oliver promised to resign his office, and not to deal in any stamps in the meantime. Adams then started a smear campaign against Hutchinson, saying that he himself had proposed the Stamp Act and sent his suggestions to London. Within a fortnight the mob duly sacked Hutchinson's house. Their violence was excessive, and his plight began to attract sympathy in Boston. Sam Adams therefore fabricated a story, for general circulation by word of mouth, that during the despoliation of Hutchinson's house incriminating papers had been found which proved that Hutchinson had originally formulated the Stamp Act.

These papers were never produced, because they did not exist. Adams was beginning to explore the intricacies of successful propaganda.

ADAMS RULES THE MOBS

In the reaction to the violence attending the sack of Hutchinson's house, the leader of one of the two Boston mobs, Andrew Mackintosh, was imprisoned. Adams got him released. The Caucus even obtained for him a post of profit in the municipal service. But Adams's price was that Mackintosh should unite the rival Boston gangs, and that the united mob should act in future in a far more disciplined manner, responding only to the orders of Sam Adams, which were now transmitted through Mackintosh and enforced by a most efficient corps of intermediate storm-troop-leaders.

The organised Boston mob now became an official body, the Sons of Liberty, which virtually held all civil power in the town. As a demonstration of strength they forced Andrew Oliver to renew publicly at the Liberty Tree his oath that he would never enforce the Stamp Act in America. Adams then declared the Stamp Act void in Massachusetts, and all normal business and litigation went on without payment of tax. The Caucus successfully pushed through a town meeting their demand that Hutchinson, himself (among other offices) a Judge of Probate, should run the business

The true Sons of Liberty

And Supporters of the Non-Importation Agreement,

ARE determined to reſent any the leaſt Inſult or Menace offer'd to any one or more of the ſeveral Committees appointed by the Body at Faneuil-Hall, and chaſtiſe any one or more of them as they deſerve; and will alſo ſupport the Printers in any Thing the Committees ſhall deſire them to print.

☞ AS a Warning to any one that ſhall affront as aforeſaid, upon ſure Information given, one of theſe Advertiſements will be poſted up at the Door or Dwelling-Houſe of the Offender.

Adams used open intimidation to keep his policies progressing at speed.
MANSELL COLLECTION

of his Court without imposing the stamp tax. Unable to defy the force against him, Hutchinson resigned his office as Judge. Massachusetts then called an intercolonial congress to petition the King against the formal continuance of the Stamp Act.

Plans were made for 40,000 New Englanders to confront the British Army forces expected to be drafted in to overcome their rebellious opposition. But before blood was shed in any pitched battle, the British Government repealed the Stamp Act, probably intimidated less by prospective rebellion than by the commercial effects of a damaging colonial boycott on British goods. But at the same time the government passed a Declaratory Act maintaining that they had a solid right to tax the American Colonies.

PRINCE OF PROPAGANDA

Before the Stamp Act agitation Sam Adams had been a busy but little regarded trouble-maker, holding a minor post as collector of taxes in which he had failed so miserably that his accounts were several thousand pounds in arrear – the result, his enemies alleged, of embezzlement by Adams. After the victory of 1766 Adams set himself to consolidate himself as a leader of the Whig Party in Massachusetts, and to extend the influence of that party. He controlled the *Boston Gazette* newspaper, and converted it into a revolutionary organ. His skilful propaganda included the then novel tactic of printing in his newspaper the names of all Tories voting against controversial measures 'so as to mark the Nays for resentment (that is, mob retaliation)'. By publicity and intimidation he won for the Whigs the 1766 election for the House of Representatives, and was himself elected Clerk to the House. His immense persuasive skill was thus directed to composing the drafts of Massachusetts petitions to King George, and representations to the King's Minister. His control of the press enabled him to publish – against all precedent – what were often inter-departmental Colonial Office memos as soon as they were composed. When it was objected that the public could read these fiery protests before even they had reached the Minister, he scoffed, 'You know it was designed for the People, and not for the Minister.'

Sam Adams had a depth and sincerity of purpose, an ancient Puritan fire, and above all a novel, positive revolutionary philosophy, which earned him high respect and numerous disciples among the 'intellectuals' of

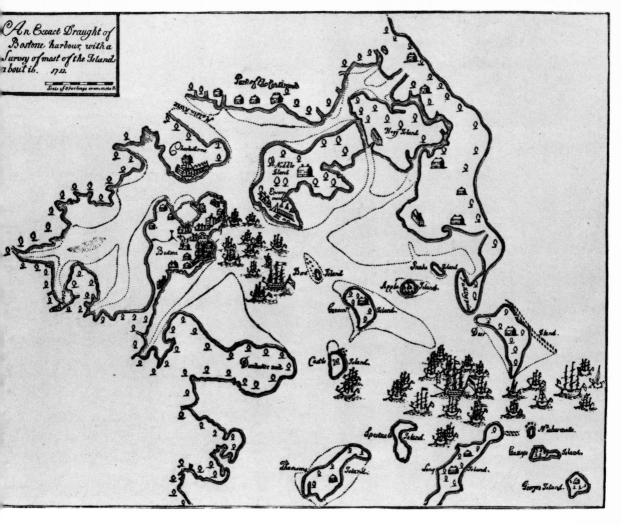

'An Exact Draught of Boston Harbour
with a Survey of most of the islands
about it, 1733.'
J. G. MOORE COLLECTION

Massachusetts. These men were not ashamed to call themselves the Sons
of Liberty, though they tended to withdraw from the scene when the more
violent – and much more drunken – mobsters among the Sons of Liberty
got down to the serious wreckage and looting that was an integral part
of a Boston riot. Adams did command the allegiance of high-principled
men – but he relied on his instinctive rapport with denser legionnaires and
always had a broader entertainment to offer them. He was by no means
totally devious or irrevocably slick. But in addition to his printed propaganda he developed a visual and emotional persuasion which can be com-

129

pared only to the rallies and military circuses organised for Hitler before the Second World War. He had an instinctive mastery of the gut-reaction effected by parades and spectacular staged processions. He organised patriotic holiday celebrations with marches by the Sons of Liberty, much feasting and constant reliance on the drinking, bonfires, fireworks of un-paralleled magnitude, and the deep unthinking euphoria of popular music. To this he added his own precursor to Hitler's maniacal ravings against the Jews. Adams included in his demonstrations a savage tirade against the hidden enemies of Massachusetts and England, the ever active and ceaselessly treacherous Papists.

It was all nominally directed towards 'patriotism' – in Sam Adams's eccentric interpretation of that word – which was an exaggeration of John Wilkes's hypocritical deference towards King George III, and opposition to his government, with the implication that the King wanted to do right by his subjects, but the ministers were abusing the King by forcing legislation that he formally approved only through punctilious regard for his constitutional duties.

THE KING CALLED THE TUNE

It was a convenient ploy, and Adams never gave a moment's credence to its theoretical basis. Now that all the records have been exposed to the light of history, we know that it was King George III who was always pushing his ministers to re-establish full authority over America. The King had termed the repeal of the Stamp Act 'this fatal compliance'. Two years later, one of his ministers re-attempted compliance with the King's wishes rather than those of the Americans. In May 1767 the Chancellor of the Exchequer, Charles Townshend, 'saw that he should most readily increase his own importance by acquiescing in the wishes of the King'. He therefore intro-duced measures to tax the American Colonies, not in so direct a manner as the old Stamp Act, but by introducing the direct tax on various products exported by Great Britain to America. The most important commodity concerned was tea.

Sam Adams resisted the Townshend Duties and the Customs Com-missioners who had been drafted in to enforce collection of the new imposts. He at first restrained the Sons of Liberty from rioting, since he was trying to impress the leaders of other colonies, such as John Dickinson of Pennsylvania, known as 'The Farmer', who were disgusted by the use of

Townshend had a bright idea: the tax on tea.
MARY EVANS COLLECTION

mobs. Instead, Adams worked through his House of Representatives. Petitions to the King and to the Secretary of State for the Colonies were followed by the composition (by Adams) of a circular letter sent by the Massachusetts House of Representatives to all other American Assemblies denying the right of the British Parliament to impose external taxes for the purpose of raising revenue rather than controlling trade.

MILITARY OCCUPATION

Lord Hillsborough, chosen as a hard-liner to be King George's new Secretary of State, instructed the colonial Assemblies to ignore the Massachusetts circular, and commanded the Massachusetts House of Representatives to withdraw it. This peremptory order was fierily refused in a historic debate which roused the enthusiasm of other American colonies, already sensitive under Hillsborough's dragooning. Hillsborough suspended the Massachusetts House of Representatives for an indefinite period. Sam Adams merely called more frequent town's meetings in Boston, engineered a riot or two, and finally summoned a Massachusetts Convention, which was little more than the banned Assembly under another name.

At last there was a full-scale riot in Boston, on 10 June 1768, which expelled the Commissioners of the Customs from the town. George III had just had to face home rioting on his own doorstep in troublesome connection with the defiant return to Great Britain of John Wilkes. To punish

131

Lord Hillsborough suspended the
Massachusetts House of Representatives.
MARY EVANS COLLECTION

*John Stuart, the 3rd Earl of Bute
(1713–92), was reputed to be the lover
of George III's mother.*

'Life, Liberty and the Pursuit of Happiness' declared the New World.

Boston for its rioting, which the King thought a more manageable proposition, George III ordered that regiments of British soldiers should be sent into the town, some sailing from Ireland and some from Halifax, Nova Scotia. The Boston Sons of Liberty (through its literate Committee) complained vociferously of this tyranny to John Wilkes in London, with whom they were now in correspondence. In Boston, Adams had enough influence with the Massachusetts Convention to get a motion passed rejecting the right of the King to impose a standing army on the colony without obtaining the consent of its (suspended) Parliament. He was less successful in inciting the country yeomen – all with the reputation of being sharpshooters – to support the Boston mob in violent resistance to the British soldiers when they arrived.

THE POLITICS OF MASSACRE

The regiments landed without serious incident. Boston was militarily subdued. The mobs were temporarily silenced. King George III established an old right to have Americans suspected of treason sent to England for trial, and set his attorney-general in Boston taking affidavits to justify the transportation of Sam Adams to the Tower of London. Adams for his part began printing a series of atrocity stories against the British, daily accusing them of brutality and rape. The Liberty Boys brawled discreetly with individual soldiers. It was the beginning of a campaign of provocation that, for propaganda purposes, had to end in a massacre. The Boston Massacre (in which five people died) on 5 March 1770 was a deliberately engineered duplicate of the St George's Fields Massacre (in which seven died) in London on 10 May 1768 – well-known to Adams if only because of his connection with Wilkes, who was the unwilling focus of the London killings. In Boston, Sam Adams intended deaths to occur, and tried to make the most of them. In this ploy, particularly in an attempt to stage a show-trial of British redcoats, he was largely to fail. Sam Adams turned to higher levels of persuasion, the intellectual circles of the patriots in England. He reached for his pen and wrote a powerful emotional and informative letter to John Wilkes, to welcome him to freedom after 22 months in gaol.

John Wilkes had spent the first months of his exile in Europe with an Italian mistress, Gertrude Corradini, of whom he recorded, 'She possessed the divine gift of lewdness, but nature had not given her strength adequate to the force of her desires.' In addition, Nature had not given her the grace

The Boston Massacre, 'deliberately
engineered by Adams to match the St
George's Fields Massacre involving
Wilkes.'
MARY EVANS COLLECTION

Foundlings, Soldiers, Jews

Parifian Taylors,

And Jewellers,

SOLICIT your VOTE and INTEREST for the *Immaculate*

John Wilkes, Efq.

To be CHAMBERLAIN of this CITY.

of constancy, and she left him in Naples, taking in her baggage all the valuables that could be conveniently removed from the house they shared. Wilkes returned to Paris, and when George III had to appoint a Whig ministry after impatiently dismissing the ineffectual Grenville, Wilkes fully expected to receive an official pardon, an annulment of his outlawry, and a lucrative ambassadorship. But no offer was made to him, either in this or the ensuing ministry. Wilkes endured in acute poverty, and finally decided to return to England and contest the general election due to be held in Spring 1768, seven years after his previous success at Aylesbury.

He entered England openly. He even sent his footman to Buckingham Palace with a letter to the King asking for a formal pardon. The King indignantly spurned the message, but he did not order Wilkes's arrest. Wilkes offered himself for one of the four parliamentary seats in the City of London. He was rapturously received by the common people, and generously welcomed by many of the more affluent, who started a subscription fund to pay his debts. But he had allowed insufficient time for canvassing, and came bottom of the poll.

Immediately he offered himself for the constituency of Middlesex, where the poll had not yet been taken. Middlesex, which included much of urban London outside Westminster, had a comparatively full and democratic register of electors. Though there were only five days of electioneering remaining, Wilkes's enthusiastic supporters placarded the constituency with his symbol – the number 45 – and escorted him triumphantly to the hustings. He came top of the poll.

London was enveloped in a wild bout of celebration which lasted two days. The King called out the army to restore order, but was appalled to hear that even some of the regimental drummers were 'beating for Wilkes'. Even, in fact, George's heir, later to be the Prince Regent. For the Prince of Wales caught a boyish intimation of how to insult his father, and climaxed a family quarrel by shouting 'Wilkes and No. 45 for ever!' – and sprinting fast out of the breakfast room. So great was this sudden clamour

Wilkes returned to London, and the King called out the Army to restore order. 'But even some of the regimental drummers were beating for Wilkes.'

MARY EVANS COLLECTION

138

for Wilkes after four years' absence that the American Benjamin Franklin noted the possibility that Wilkes could be nominated as King.

Having secured his seat in Parliament, Wilkes, as he had promised, surrendered to the Court of the King's Bench to appeal against his sentence of outlawry. Lord Mansfield, unwilling to face mob action for sentencing him for the original libels, declared that Wilkes had not yet been properly arrested, and told him to go away. Wilkes waited a week. Nobody arrested him. He requested a sheriff's officer to do so, and then wrote formally to the Attorney General with the information that he had arranged his own arrest and was requesting judgment. Wilkes was consigned to the King's Bench Prison in St George's Fields, but an ecstatic mob rescued him from the black maria. Wilkes excused himself, knocked at the prison door, and asked to be admitted.

John Wilkes before the court of the King's Bench. From the Gentleman's Magazine *of 1768.*
J. G. MOORE COLLECTION

MURDER APPROVED

For a fortnight the London crowds surged round the King's Bench Prison serenading their hero within. The government was infuriated, and ordered military action. In the foreseen confrontation the soldiers fired, and six demonstrators were killed. A patrol of a Scottish regiment yielded to passion and, some distance from the scene of the action, shot dead an innocent citizen. The King grimly welcomed the deed and pumped his prestige into the outcome. The Secretary at War declared, 'His Majesty highly approves of the conduct of both officers and men. They shall have every defence and protection that the law can authorise and this office can give.' The trial of the soldiers for murder was switched from London to Guildford, and a packed Grand Jury threw out the bill.

At the King's Bench hearing of Wilkes's appeal against outlawry, Lord Mansfield found a convenient technical error in the original proceedings, and declared that the writ of outlawry was void. This time it was not only

*Lord Chief Justice Mansfield found a
convenient technical error and annuled
Wilkes's outlawry.*

IOHN GLYNN
Esq.
Serjeant at Law.

London, but the principal cities of England, which exploded into un-
controlled mass celebration. Ten days later, Wilkes appeared for sentence
on the original libel charges. He was fined £1000, which his supporters
immediately paid, and sentenced to 22 months in prison. He served his
confinement in the utmost available luxury. He was inundated with gifts of
food and wine, money and women – for he had the utmost freedom in
receiving friends and lovers.

Wilkes was still a Member of Parliament. George III decided that that situation was impossible. 'The expulsion of Mr Wilkes appears to be very essential and must be effected,' he instructed his Prime Minister. But in the meantime Wilkes was busy. He wrote an inflammatory pamphlet on the St George's Fields Massacre. He presented to Parliament a general petition against his treatment during the lengthy episodes of the prosecutions for No. 45 and *An Essay on Woman*. And this, by parliamentary rule, had to be heard. In addition Wilkes was elected, in his absence in prison, an alderman of the City of London. And his talented supporter, the lawyer Serjeant Glynn, was successful in a bye-election in being returned as his fellow-member of Parliament for Middlesex. At this election there occurred an extraordinary parliamentary innovation. Wilkes and Glynn were given – and they accepted – instructions from their constituents to pursue a five-point political programme. It was the first 'mandate' ever acceded to by

The murder, far away from St George's Fields, of Allen which, said the Secretary at War, 'The King highly approves.'
MANSELL COLLECTION

any British Member of Parliament, the first 'platform' ever delineated as the aims of a political party.

Wilkes duly presented his petition to Parliament, but it was so efficiently castrated by the law officers of the Crown that only two weak points of argument remained, and the petition was rejected. Next day, Wilkes attended the Commons to resist King George's motion for his expulsion. The concocted ground for this action had been that he had libelled the Government in his pamphlet on the St George's Fields Massacre. To this the King forced the additional charges that he had written the seditious and obscene libels of No. 45 and *An Essay on Woman* – actions for which he had already been expelled from Parliament four years previously, had subsequently been heavily fined, and was now suffering imprisonment. The combination of criminal and moral charges was sufficient, as the King had foreseen, to secure a majority in favour of his expulsion. But what may have seemed to the King an immediate victory was the deluding image of his final defeat. By one ill-judged action of irrational personal revenge he had raised in the mind of the nation the questions of the overweening arrogance not only of the Crown, but also of Parliament, encroaching on the liberty of decision of the electors.

The principal toughs hired to oppose Wilkite candidates at the Middlesex elections were the Irish chairmen (sedan-chair porters) . . .
MARY EVANS COLLECTION

. . . but it was all right on the night.
MARY EVANS COLLECTION

EXPULSION INFINITE

Wilkes was delighted to raise this issue in the election address which he immediately published – for he stood as candidate for Middlesex at the ensuing bye-election. He was returned unopposed, with 2000 ready to speak if anyone dared contest his claim. Next day the House of Commons expelled him, and additionally declared that he was 'incapable of being a member'. The Commons decreed a fresh election, and again Wilkes was returned unopposed. The Commons declared the election null and void, and the Government put up a candidate for the fourth poll. Wilkes beat this candidate, Colonel Henry Luttrell, with a four-to-one majority. But the Commons not only declared this election null and void, they decreed that Luttrell 'ought to have been elected' and inscribed him as the Member for Middlesex.

The popular disgust which had accompanied this five-weeks farce had deepened to the point where the rallying cry in the streets was now 'Wilkes

ENGLISH LIBERTY established, or a MIRROUR for POSTERITY:
JOHN WILKES, Esq.r the undaunted ASSERTOR of the LIBERTY of the PRESS,
and the RIGHTS of ENGLISH-MEN.

Warmed with the love of freedom & his Country.
He hears their threats unmov'd.
And with superior greatness smiles.

Englishmen freed from the Fear of General Warrants,
and the Seizure of Papers, by the Magnanimity of
ONE MAN.

Mansion House.
wilkes on return from Guild Hall. 21 March. 1768.
And the People delight to honour him.

Publish'd according to Act of Parliament. May 1768

To the Gentlemen, Clergy, and Freeholders of the County of Middlesex, and the Liverymen of the City of London, who voted for
Mr. WILKES, and to all the Sons of Liberty, this Plate is inscrib'd.

Tribute to a popular hero.

Wilkes's come-back with a Derry-down-derry.

THE FLIGHT OF LIBERTY.

THE RETURN OF LIBERTY.

publiſhed as the Act directs by J. Williams Nᵒ 38. Fleet Street. Price 6 1768

LIBERTY REVIVED.

Tenax propoſiti.

I.

WHEN BUTE and his Faction had ravag'd the Land,
And Old *Engliſh* Liberty hardly could ſtand,
Then WILKES, the TRUE CHAMPION of FREEDOM, aroſe,
Determin'd to combat his Country's dread Foes.
Derry Down, &c.

II.

Notwithſtanding their Power, their Craft, and their Spite,
Their Turning and Winding to prove Wrong was Right,
For his Country's Good ſtill reſolv'd to proceed,
He defy'd the bare Bums that came wigging from *Tweed.*

III.

When they found him ſo ſtaunch in his Country's Cauſe,
To each one explaining the Senſe of our Laws,
They rav'd, and they rag'd, and they made a great Pother,
And ſtar'd, like *Jack Puddings*, each one at the other.

IV.

Strait a Party was formed by SAWNEY the *Scot*;
By St. *Andrew* they ſwore, that WILKES ſhould go to pot;
Yet, in ſpite of their Malice and d—'d Combination,
He his Honour maintained to all their Vexation.

V.

D—N, M—N and K—L, the Scum of the Nation,
By Perjury, Fraud, and by Aſſaſſination,
With a B—ſh—p, a J—dge, fully bent on his Fall,
Got *England*'s Friend baniſh'd for—nothing at all.

VI.

Britannia was ſad when ſhe heard of his Fate,
And LIBERTY groan'd at her wofull Eſtate:
In vain did they groan, and in vain did they ſigh,
In vain was their Sorrow, for WILKES was not by.

VII.

At laſt he's return'd to his own native Iſle,
And the Genius of *Britain* comes forth with a Smile :
FREEDOM lifts up her Head, crown'd with Laurels again ;
For WILKES, ſhe is ſure, will her Honour maintain.

VIII.

Ye Livery of *London*, mind what you're about ;
Think who ſhould be in, and who ſhould be out :
On your Choice now your City, your Charter depend ;
And WILKES is the Man will your Freedom defend.
Derry Down, &c.

and No King!' – an astonishingly swift fulfilment of Benjamin Franklin's prophecy. The King had insisted on the expulsion of Wilkes, '*a measure whereon almost my Crown depends*', he had written to Lord Hertford. It was an absurd exaggeration of the personal importance of Wilkes at that time, but the paranoia which caused its expression, and the maintenance of that self-indulgent hatred, came near to making it a factual summary of the political importance of Wilkes, and the growing Wilkite movement, from that time.

The King actually moved into the arena of popular electioneering in order to defeat Wilkes. National support for Wilkes – and the rights of electors in relation to Parliament – was demonstrated in countless petitions organised all over England and Wales. The King thereupon ordered his agents to set up counter-petitions in support of the Crown. These in their turn stimulated reaction in Wilkite supporters who had been too timid previously to enter this novel public field. It was a stirring-up of public life, an involvement of non-voters, especially in the newer cities, who were outside the roll of the old electorate. Its effect was to stimulate the responsibility of parliamentarians to the constituents they represented, and to begin the shaping of the modern political party.

When Wilkes was finally released from the King's Bench Prison in April 1770 he did not immediately return to Parliament, having been most effectively expelled, but dedicated his activities to the City of London and to a historic campaign for the freedom of the press to report parliamentary proceedings. When the next general election came, in 1774, not only was Wilkes returned triumphantly for Middlesex, but a dozen colleagues went to the Commons with him. They were the Wilkites, a new political party, and they had an agreed programme. A significant plank in their platform was 'to redress grievances and secure the popular rights in Great Britain, Ireland and America'.

WILKES AND AMERICA STAND TOGETHER

America had followed the fine details of the King's campaign against Wilkes with the greatest sympathy. On the announcement of his imprisonment, *forty-five* hogsheads of tobacco were immediately sent to him at the King's Bench as a gift from Maryland. (Wilkes, in turn, gave them away to friends. 'I do not smoke,' he said. 'I have no *small* vices.') But it was Boston that took Wilkes to its heart – and requested his support. The Sons of Liberty were in correspondence with him even before his imprisonment,

This fanciful coat-of-arms for Wilkes is
quartered: a General Warrant torn to
rags; a bunch of broken keys denoting
the ruin of Arbitrary Power; the Tower
of London with its gates wide open.

149

and Sam Adams put his signature to their letters. When they heard of his sentence, they sent the first of many gifts. Wilkes wrote in acknowledgment from his prison on 19 July 1768 'To the Gentlemen of the Committee of the Sons of Liberty in the Town of Boston':

Gentlemen,

I am extremely honoured by your letter, and the valuable present which accompanied it. Nothing could give me more satisfaction than to find the true spirit of Liberty so generally diffus'd through the most remote parts of the British Monarchy ... As a member of the Legislature I shall always give a particular attention to whatever respects the interests of America ... After the first claims of duty to England, and of gratitude to the County of Middlesex, none shall engage me more than the affairs of our Colonies, which I consider as the *propugnacula imperii* [bulwarks of empire], and I know how much of our strength and weight we owe to, and derive from, them ... I will ever, Gentlemen, avow myself a friend to universal liberty. I hope freedom will ever flourish under your hemisphere as well as ours, and I doubt not from your spirit and firmness that you will be careful to transmit to your posterity the invaluable rights and franchises which you have received from your ancestors. Liberty I consider as the birthright of every subject of the British Empire, and I hold Magna Charta to be in as full force in America as in Europe. I hope that these truths will become generally known ... The only ambition I feel is to distinguish myself as a friend of the rights of mankind, both religious and civil, as a man zealous for the preservation of this constitution and our Sovereign, *with all our laws and native liberties that ask not his leave*, if I may use the expression of Milton ...

Sam Adams, with warmth in his Puritan heart even for a rake as notorious as Wilkes, wrote:

No Character appears with a stronger Luster in my Mind than that of a Man who nobly perseveres in the Cause of public Liberty and Virtue through the Rage of Persecution: of this you have had a large Portion; but I dare say you are made the better for it.

Wilkes wrote back with more than the dutifulness of a public figure. His letters were read aloud to the Sons of Liberty with acclamation. They replied in passages which give a genuine insight into the problems of rebellion, as encountered by not-altogether-convinced rebels. A letter was sent from the Sons of Liberty dated 5 October 1768 – it was received in the King's Bench Prison on 7 November, which is faster than the speed of sea-mail two centuries later – acknowledging Wilkes's last:

Benjamin Franklin (1706–90),
scientist, statesman and Founding Father.

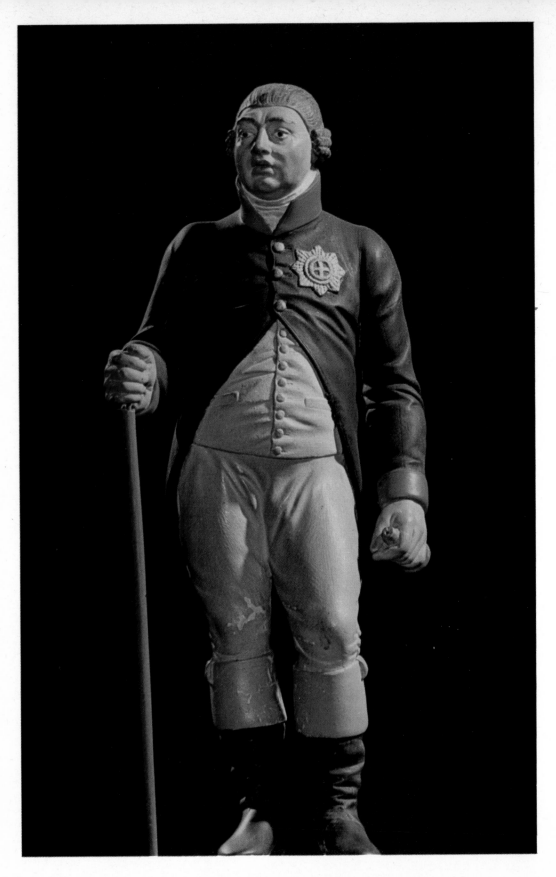

*A contemporary figurine of George III
reflecting his sobriety and piety.*
NATIONAL PORTRAIT GALLERY

Samuel Adams

The members were immediately assembled, and inexpressible was the satisfaction of our regale (banquet) on the genuine sentiments of a worthy Briton. Your health, your friends and cause were the toasts of the evening.

They asked Wilkes a question which was by no means rhetorical:

Is our reluctance to oppose Brother to Brother deemed a prospect of our submission? Or, *e contra*, is a mere presumption that indignation and despair must hurry us on to violent measures, ground sufficient to treat us with all the parade of a triumph over vanquish'd Rebels?

Thomas Young wrote to Wilkes on another occasion:

The unanimity of all the Colonies, the exhilarating advice of the increase of your party, seem to us sufficient to deter the most adventurous desperado from risquing further experiments on a people who need but a spark to set them all in flames.

The Sons of Liberty were indeed curiously dependent on advice from Wilkes, and politically bound to him by ties little recognised then or since. William Palfrey, one of the Sons of Liberty, wrote personally to Wilkes with emphasis: *The fate of Wilkes and America must stand or fall together.*

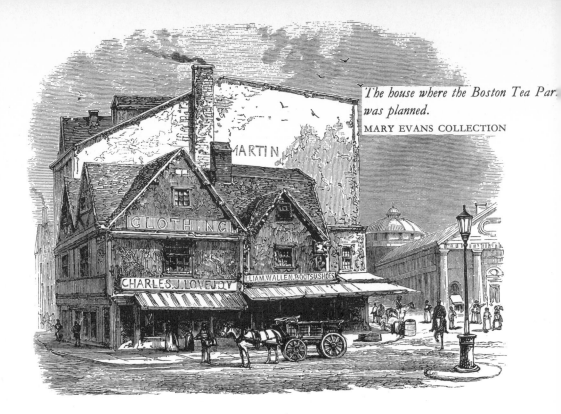

The house where the Boston Tea Party was planned.
MARY EVANS COLLECTION

CONCENTRATES THE MIND WONDERFULLY

Wilkes replied with serious application to the problems put to him. His incarceration in the King's Bench Prison – English political feuding and English lady-loves apart – gave him an opportunity perhaps otherwise unique to ponder the problems of American democracy which he expounded so effectively within Britain before the American War:

I have read with grief and indignation the proceedings of the Ministry with regard to the Troops order'd to Boston, as if it were the capital of a province belonging to our enemies. Asiatic despotism does not present a picture more odious in the eye of humanity than the sanctuary of justice and law turned into a main-guard [the Parliament House of Boston used as the British Army's advanced headquarters].

The niceties of hospitality were not neglected. William Palfrey wrote a year after Wilkes's entry into prison, when gifts might be supposed to have dwindled:

The society of the friends of Liberty have directed me to forward you two Turtle ... They are now in fine order, one weighs 45 lb., the other 47, making in the whole 92, which is the Massachusetts patriotic number.

154

Finally, Sam Adams wrote, in what must have been one of the last letters Wilkes received in prison from America, a statement of intent, a self-delineation of character, and a warning to King George III, that did not deserve to be ignored by politicians who were shortly to be press-ganged into a King's War against America:

In this little part of the World – a Land, till of late happy in its Obscurity – the Asylum to which Patriots were formerly wont to make their peaceful Retreat; even here the stern Tyrant has lifted up his iron Rod, and makes his incessant Claim as Lord of the Soil. But I have a firm Perswasion in my Mind that this Country will approve herself as glorious in defending and maintaining her Freedom as she has heretofore been happy in enjoying it.

Were I a Native and an Inhabitant of Britain and capable of affording the least Advice, it should constantly be; to confirm the Colonies in the fullest Exercise of their Rights, and ever to explore for them every possible Avenue of Trade which should not interfere with her own Manufactures. From the Colonies, when she is worn with Age, she is to expect renewed Strength. But the Field I am entering is too large for the present: May Heaven forbid that it should be truly said of Great Britain *Quam Deus vult perdere* . . .! [Whom God wishes to destroy He first makes mad].

> I am with strict truth
> Sir
> Your most humble servant
> *Samuel Adams.*

It is not extravagance to call the struggle the King's War. It is not pseudo-psychology to see in the King's deepening acceptance of obsessions, stimulated by his excessive preoccupation with Wilkes, culminating in his transference of the same personal, *unstatesmanlike*, repugnance to the Americans, a destructive madness, whether or not it was the blight of God. The brilliant anonymous pamphleteer Junius recognised as early as 19 December 1769, six years before the war was serious, the extraordinarily dependent relationship between George III, Wilkes and the American protagonists of independence. He wrote – personally but publicly – to King George:

Mr Wilkes brought with him into politics the same liberal sentiments by which his private conduct had been directed, and seemed to think that, as there are few excesses in which an English gentleman may not be permitted to indulge, the same latitude was allowed him in the choice of his political principles . . . In the earnestness of his zeal, he suffered some unwarrantable insinuations to escape him.

He said more than moderate men would justify; but not enough to entitle him to the honour of your Majesty's personal resentment. The rays of royal indignation, collected upon him, served only to illuminate, and could not consume. Animated by the favour of the people on one side, and heated by persecution on the other, his views and sentiments changed with his situation. Hardly serious at first, he is now an enthusiast. The coldest bodies warm with opposition; the hardest sparkle in collision. There is a holy mistaken zeal in politics as well as in religion. By persuading others, we convince ourselves. The passions are engaged, and create a material affection in the mind, which forces us to love the cause for which we suffer.

Is this a contention worthy of a King? Are you not sensible how much the meanness of the cause gives an air of ridicule to the serious difficulties into which you have been betrayed? The destruction of one man has now been, for many years, the sole object of your Government: and if there can be anything still more disgraceful, we have seen, for such an object, the utmost influence of the executive power, and every Ministerial artifice, exerted without success . . . [The Colonies] were ready enough to distinguish between *you* and your Ministers. They complained of an act of legislature, but traced the origin of it no higher than to the servants of the Crown. They pleased themselves with the hope that their Sovereign, if not favourable to their cause, was at least impartial. The decisive, personal part you took against them has effectually banished that first distinction from their minds. They consider you as united with your servants against America.

The part of 'personal resentment' played by George III against America led to the far more skilful, even more bitterly resentful, actions of Sam Adams, culminating in the brilliant contrivance of the provocation of the Boston Tea Party, the point in the battle of wills from which there was no return. The stage was set. The outcome was inevitable.

George III: a man with intense personal animosity.
MARY EVANS COLLECTION

WHY THE KING LOST AMERICA

In 1760 three dissimilar men in three remote stations of life were converging on a collision course that would keep them locked in battle for twenty years. They were King George III, John Wilkes, and Sam Adams. Wilkes, careless with his venom, was gratuitously wounding to King George. Because of a damaging weakness of character the King overreacted and devoped an obsessional personal vendetta against Wilkes. This gave Wilkes far more popular support than he would otherwise have received, but it also fundamentally changed Wilkes's political attitude. He became a sincere and able advocate of popular liberty.

In influential correspondence with Sam Adams and the Sons of Liberty, Wilkes led the Americans in militancy of theory. Adams provided the lead in militancy of action. King George repeated his mistake, and overreacted again, building a new vendetta against the colonists until it could be reliably reported to Adams, 'The King hates most cordially every American because he thinks they have an attachment to their Liberty.'

The King saw the Wilkite movement in Great Britain and the resistance movement in America in exactly the same light – as the work of rebels to whom no concession should be granted.

The formation of the Wilkes party, the first modern political party with a platform previously agreed with the electors, encouraged the elder Pitt

DESTRUCTION OF THE T

IN BOSTON HARBOUR.

to renew opposition to the King for his corrupt domination of Parliament. As a result, the King began a twelve-year autocracy which allowed the War of Independence to be fought and lost on the terms the King dictated.

The Wilkites supported American democracy. Adams personally urged Wilkes to make the rights of the American colonies the major theme of his programme. Adams publicly developed his theme that the King was bound by natural laws 'antecedent and paramount to all positive Laws of Man'. He spoke of 'an appeal to Heaven' against George III. In a skilful progression of his propaganda technique, he slowly undermined the built-in awe felt for the King. Alongside the intellectual arguments, Adams achieved his greatest coup in deliberately building a war psychosis by his masterly management of the Boston Tea Party.

The King replied with four punitive Acts of Parliament aimed at Massachusetts and Boston. Massachusetts defied the King and his army of occupation, and called out the State militia. The King ordered Sam Adams to be hanged as soon as he was caught.

Sam Adams is not to be so exalted that he must be given all credit for the formation of the United States, nor the King so denigrated that he is deemed to have lost an empire single-handed. But it was Sam Adams who was early called by Governor Hutchinson 'the great incendiary leader'. Royalist Americans termed the Revolution 'Adams's conspiracy'; Lord North called the revolutionists 'Sam Adams's crew,' and King George specifically excluded Adams from the general amnesty offered before the start of the war. At the other pole, it was the personal animosity of George III that gave the colonial leaders their eventual solidarity as the despised and therefore self-conscious 'Americans', created before they really existed through the King's insistence on constructing bogey men.

Obsessively inflexible, George III never altered his thinking about America. Before hostilities, he wanted unconditional subjection of the American people in advance of any discussion of terms. Once the King had to fight the war, he laid down this maxim for all incoming Ministers, 'Before I will even hear of any man's readiness to come into office I will expect to see it signed under his hand that he is resolved to keep the empire entire, and that no troops shall be consequently drawn from America, nor independence *ever* allowed.' Originally he had mistakenly thought that he would give the Americans 'a few bloody noses' and, having reduced the rebels to prostrate submission, would call off his bruisers without even designating the operation as a war. When he saw

HOUSE OF HANOVER
GEORGE III,
Began his Reign Oct.ᵗ 25 1760

Phillips Sc.

George III. 'Heaven forbid,' said
Adams, 'that it should be said "Whom
God wishes to destroy he first makes
mad." '

MARY EVANS COLLECTION

161

his error, he adopted a bitter policy of wilful prolongation, blockade, strangulation of trade, and marginal devastation by seaborne raiders and hired Indians. There was no thought of political concession, and this meant, paradoxically, that he had already conceded defeat. 'Every means of distressing America must meet with my concurrence,' he said, while he turned to conduct new wars with France, Spain, Holland and the Northern Alliance. What George III had intended as a rap on an American head from the baton of a martinet had developed into a war of the great powers, which the King enthusiastically entered, *although that was precisely the situation he had been trying to avoid when he first came to the throne.*

King George's failure in his struggle against Adams and America is inextricably bound up with his failure against Wilkes and popular liberty. His paranoid personal involvement in political feuds was exercised and developed against Wilkes, and beat itself to death against Adams.

In the end, by 1783, George, Wilkes and Adams were all destroyed as personal forces, and they all lived on in impotence. Yet something of what they had fought for existed – Adams's American Independence, but not under his leadership; Wilkes's liberty for strident demagogues, which was a beginning for democracy; even George's early ambition to cleanse the political pig-sty. For he had purged the political life of the country in one aspect. He had smashed the entirely self-centred corruption of the Whig families, and he had set Britain on a course of stable, if authoritarian, government which at least sailed her through the hurricane of the French Revolution, and on to Trafalgar and Waterloo.

Three human beings, almost irresistible forces, had converged and finally collided. Their lieutenants and successors came out of the clash in fairly good order. But when these three called a personal muster, all physical and emotional integrity had disappeared. Yet they could not blink the outcome – between them, these three had fired the creation of modern America.

The Declaration of Independence

THE FIRST CONTINENTAL CONGRESS ON 11 JUNE 1776 APPOINTED JOHN Adams, Thomas Jefferson, Benjamin Franklin, Roger Sherman and Robert L. Livingston to draft a Declaration of Independence. The Declaration, primarily the work of Thomas Jefferson, was adopted by the Continental Congress in Philadelphia on 4 July 1776. Since then that date has been the chief American political holiday – Independence Day.

Upon its adoption, a copy of the Declaration, inscribed on parchment, was signed by fifty-six Members of Congress on and after 2 August 1776. The original parchment document, with signatures, is now on public view in an hermetically sealed, helium-filled glass case in the National Archives Building, Washington D.C.

*Independence is proclaimed throughout the
American Colonies.*

The
Declaration
of
Independence

WHEN in the Course of Human Events it becomes necessary for one people to dissolve the political bands which have connected them with another, and to assume among the Powers of the earth, the separate and equal station to which the Laws of Nature and of Nature's God entitle them, a decent respect to the opinions of mankind requires that they should declare the causes which impel them to the separation.

We hold these truths to be self-evident, that all men are created equal, that they are endowed by their Creator with certain unalienable Rights, that among these are Life, Liberty and the pursuit of Happiness.

That to secure these rights, Governments are instituted among Men, deriving their just powers from the consent of the governed, That whenever any Form of Government becomes destructive of these ends, it is the Right of the People to alter or to abolish it, and to institute a new Government, laying its foundation on such principles, and organizing its powers in such form, as to them shall seem most likely to effect their Safety and Happiness. Prudence, indeed, will dictate that Governments long established should not be changed for light and transient causes; and accordingly all experience hath shown, that mankind are more disposed to suffer, while evils are sufferable, than to right themselves by abolishing the forms to which they are accustomed. But when a long train of abuses and usurpations, pursuing invariably the same Object evinces a design to reduce them under absolute Despotism, it is their right, it is their duty, to throw off such Government, and to provide new Guards for their future security.—Such has been the patient sufferance of these Colonies; and such is now the necessity which constrains them to alter their former Systems of Government. The history of the present King of Great Britain is a history of repeated injuries and usurpations, all having in direct object the establishment of an absolute Tyranny over these States. To prove this, let Facts be submitted to a candid world.

He has refused his Assent to Laws, the most wholesome and necessary for the public good.

He has forbidden his Governors to pass Laws of immediate and pressing importance, unless suspended in their operation till his Assent should be obtained; and when so suspended, he has utterly neglected to attend to them.

He has refused to pass other Laws for the accommodation of large districts of people, unless those people would relinquish the right of Representation in the Legislature, a right inestimable to them and formidable to tyrants only.

He has called together legislative bodies at places unusual, uncomfortable, and distant from the depository of their Public Records, for the sole purpose of fatiguing them into compliance with his measures.

He has dissolved Representative Houses repeatedly, for opposing with manly firmness his invasions on the rights of the people.

He has refused for a long time, after such dissolutions, to cause others to be elected; whereby the Legislative Powers, incapable of Annihilation, have returned to the People at large for their exercise; the State remaining in the mean time exposed to all the dangers of invasion from without, and convulsions within.

He has endeavoured to prevent the population of these States; for that purpose obstructing the Laws of Naturalization of Foreigners; refusing to pass others to encourage their migrations hither, and raising the conditions of new Appropriations of Lands.

He has obstructed the Administration of Justice, by refusing his Assent to Laws for establishing Judiciary Powers.

He has made Judges dependent on his Will alone, for the tenure of their offices, and the amount and payment of their salaries.

He has erected a multitude of New Offices, and sent hither swarms of Officers to harrass our People, and eat out their substance.

He has kept among us, in times of peace, Standing Armies without the Consent of our legislature.

He has affected to render the Military independent of and superior to the Civil Power.

He has combined with others to subject us to a jurisdiction foreign to our constitution, and unacknowledged by our laws; giving his Assent to their acts of pretended legislation: For quartering large bodies of armed troops among us: For protecting them, by a mock Trial, from Punishment for any Murders which they should commit on the Inhabitants of these States: For cutting off our trade with all parts of the world: For imposing Taxes on us without our Consent: For depriving us in many cases, of the benefits of Trial by Jury: For transporting us beyond Seas to be tried for pretended offences: For abolishing the free System of English Laws in a neighbouring Province, establishing therein an Arbitrary government, and enlarging its Boundaries so as to render it at once an example and fit instrument for introducing the same absolute rule into these Colonies: For taking away our Charters, abolishing our most valuable Laws, and altering fundamentally the Forms of our Governments: For suspending our own Legislature, and declaring themselves invested with Power to legislate for us in all cases whatsoever.

He has abdicated Government here, by declaring us out of his Protection and waging War against us.

He has plundered our seas, ravaged our Coasts, burnt our towns, and destroyed the lives of our people.

The Declaration of Independence, endorsed by all thirteen States, was ratified by the Continental Congress on 4 July 1776.

Sam Adams: 'in the end, destroyed as a personal force.'
MANSELL COLLECTION

He is at this time transporting large armies of foreign mercenaries to compleat the works of death, desolation and tyranny, already begun with circumstances of Cruelty and perfidy scarcely paralleled in the most barbarous ages, and totally unworthy the Head of a civilized nation.

He has constrained our fellow Citizens taken Captive on the high Seas to bear Arms against their Country, to become the executioners of their friends and Brethren, or to fall themselves by their Hands.

He has excited domestic insurrections amongst us, and has endeavoured to bring on the inhabitants of our frontiers, the merciless Indian Savages, whose known rule of warfare, is an undistinguished destruction of all ages, sexes and conditions.

In every stage of these Oppressions We have Petitioned for Redress in the most humble terms: Our repeated Petitions have been answered only by repeated injury. A Prince, whose character is thus marked by every act which may define a Tyrant, is unfit to be the ruler of a free People.

Nor have We been wanting in attentions to our British brethren. We have warned them from time to time of attempts by their legislature to extend an unwarrantable jurisdiction over us. We have reminded them of the circumstances of our emigration and settlement here. We have appealed to their native justice and magnanimity, and we have conjured them by the ties of our common kindred to disavow these usurpations, which, would inevitably interrupt our connections and correspondence. They too have been deaf to the voice of justice and of consanguinity. We must, therefore, acquiesce in the necessity, which denounces our Separation, and hold them, as we hold the rest of mankind, Enemies in War, in Peace Friends.

We, therefore, the Representatives of the UNITED STATES OF AMERICA, in General Congress, Assembled, appealing to the Supreme Judge of the world for the rectitude of our intentions, do, in the Name, and by Authority of the good People of these Colonies, solemnly publish and declare, That these United Colonies are, and of Right ought to be FREE AND INDEPENDENT STATES; that they are Absolved from all Allegiance to the British Crown, and that all political connection between them and the State of Great Britain, is and ought to be totally dissolved; and that as FREE AND INDEPENDENT STATES, they have full Power to levy War, conclude Peace, contract Alliances, establish Commerce, and to do all other Acts and Things which Independent States may of right do. And for the support of this Declaration, with a firm reliance on the Protection of Divine Providence, we mutually pledge to each other our Lives, our Fortunes and our sacred Honor.

John Hancock

John Adams	*Stephen Hopkins*	*George Ross*
Samuel Adams	*Francis Hopkinson*	*Benjamin Rush*
Josiah Bartlett	*Samuel Huntington*	*Edward Rutledge*
Carter Braxton	*Thomas Jefferson*	*Roger Sherman*
Charles Carroll of	*Francis Lightfoot Lee*	*James Smith*
Carrollton	*Richard Henry Lee*	*Richard Stockton*
Samuel Chase	*Francis Lewis*	*Thomas Stone*
Abraham Clark	*Philip Livingston*	*George Taylor*
George Clymer	*Thomas Lynch, Jr.*	*Matthew Thornton*
William Ellery	*Arthur Middleton*	*George Walton*
William Floyd	*Thomas M'Kean*	*William Whipple*
Benjamin Franklin	*Lewis Morris*	*William Williams*
Elbridge Gerry	*Robert Morris*	*James Wilson*
Button Gwinnett	*John Morton*	*John Witherspoon*
Lyman Hall	*Thomas Nelson, Jr.*	*Oliver Wolcott*
Benjamin Harrison	*William Paca*	*George Wythe*
John Hart	*Robert Treat Paine*	
Joseph Hewes	*John Penn*	
Thomas Heyward, Jr.	*George Read*	
William Hooper	*Caesar Rodney*	

Chronology

1760

Accession of George III who was intent on breaking the aristocratic supremacy of the Whig Party in Parliament established during the reigns of George I and George II. Certain members were subsidised and became notorious as the 'King's Friends'.

1761

Writs of Assistance were renewed by the British Parliament enabling customs officials to avail themselves of constabulary aid when searching private property for contraband. In Massachusetts this was viewed as a threat to prosperity and as a violation of American 'natural rights'. A 'Rage for Patriotism' was generated and led by James Otis and Sam Adams.

Pitt resigned in protest at the humiliating terms of the treaty that was to end the Seven Years War with France.

1762

Bute became Prime Minister though he was popularly hated.

John Wilkes joined the opposition to George III and Bute in condemnation of the proposed peace treaty but also on a radical platform of the freedom of the press.

1763

The Peace of Paris was signed.

Grenville replaced Bute as Prime Minister.

1764

The Sugar Act and the Currency Act were two ill-conceived measures endorsed by Grenville. The first was designed to raise money to finance British troops in the colonies, and the second, to protect British mercantile interests at the expense of American trade.

The American colonists burn a revenue schooner.
MARY EVANS COLLECTION

1765

The Stamp Act, designed to raise further revenue, set in motion the revolutionary machinery by which the colonies ultimately separated from England.

Sons of Liberty groups, led by Sam Adams, were formed in Boston, New York and other towns to oppose the Stamp Act.

Rockingham replaced Grenville as Prime Minister.

1766

The Stamp Act was repealed.

The Declaratory Act was passed by Parliament 'to bind the colonies in all cases whatsoever'.

Lord Chatham (Pitt) became Prime Minister but shortly resigned because of illness and was replaced by Grafton.

1767

The Townshend Acts imposed new revenue duties and compounded use of the Writs of Assistance.

1768

The Massachusetts Circular Letter, written by Sam Adams, summarized colonial opposition to British Acts and urged colonial action. It condemned British taxation, insisted that representation in Parliament was impossible, and opposed British efforts to pay colonial governors.

Rioting in Boston as a mob attacked customs officials who tried to collect Townshend Duties from the sloop, *Liberty*, led to the stationing of British troops there.

The Virginia Association, a non-importation agreement, was organized by Sam Adams to force Britain to modify the Townshend Duties.

1769

The Virginia Resolves, denouncing British taxation in the colonies, were written in reply to the House of Lords' proposal (with which George III concurred) that the Massachusetts rebels be tried for treason.

1770

Lord North became Prime Minister.

The Boston Massacre, in which British soldiers fired into a mob, resulted in the death of five Bostonians.

The Townshend Duties, except those on tea, were repealed and non-importation by the colonies was abandoned.

1771

This was a year of comparative peace in the increasing struggle between the colonies and Great Britain.

1772

A Boston town meeting, led by Sam Adams, denounced the British policy of paying colonial officials from the Exchequer, thereby making them immune from legislative control.

Massachusetts Committees of Correspondence were established by James Otis and Sam Adams to communicate with other towns and colonies.

1773

The Tea Act was passed to save the East India Company from bankruptcy. Its tea was now the cheapest in the colonies. American importers, smugglers and the Sons of Liberty united against this Act.

The Boston Tea Party comprised a band of men disguised as Indians and led by Sam Adams who boarded ships and threw 342 chests of tea into Boston harbour.

1774

Four Coercive Acts from the British Administration produced Thomas Jefferson's *A Summary View of the Rights of British America*, which rejected the power of Parliament and claimed that colonists need only obey the king.

The first Continental Congress met in Philadelphia. (Delegates included Sam Adams for Massachusetts). It adopted a Declaration of Rights and Resolves, condemning the Coercive Acts, the revenue acts, and the standing army, and listed the rights of the colonists to include, 'life, liberty and property'. Britain, a 'foreign power', could regulate only the external commerce of the colonies.

1775

The Declaration of the First Continental Congress was laid before Parliament where a heavy majority supported the warlike policies of George III.

Lord North's Plan of Conciliation was adopted, whereby Parliament would tax no colony that would help with imperial expenses.

General Gage was ordered to use force to break up rebellion in New England.

Battles of Lexington and Concord (April).

*After the Boston Tea Party the King
ordered that Sam Adams should be
hanged as soon as he was caught.*
MARY EVANS COLLECTION

The Second Continental Congress met and voted to raise an army by requesting troops from the colonies.

Battle of Bunker Hill (June).

George III proclaimed the colonies to be in open rebellion (August).

1776
The Declaration of Independence was endorsed by all 13 states. Jefferson listed a 'long train of abuses' by George III that justified independence.

1777
Burgoyne surrendered at Saratoga.

1778
France joined the United States against Great Britain.

1781
Defeat of Cornwallis at the Siege of Yorktown.

1782
The Preliminary Articles of Peace, recognizing American independence, were drawn up.

1783
The Peace of Paris finally certified the above.

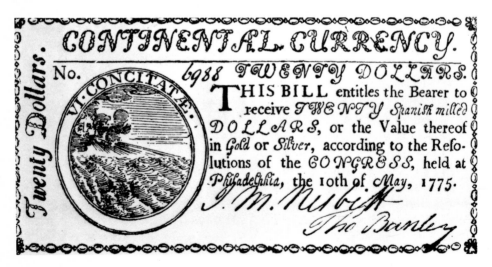

American twenty dollar bill of 1775.
J. G. MOORE COLLECTION

Select Bibliography

I. GEORGE III

BROOKE, JOHN, *King George III*, London, 1792. A detailed and highly reliable analysis of the character of George III. A standard work.

SEDGWICK, ROMNEY (editor), *The Letters from George III to Lord Bute, 1757–66*, London, 1939. The Introduction to this edition of the King's correspondence vividly sets out the relationship of George III's character to the political situation.

MCKELVEY, JAMES L., *George III and Lord Bute: The Leicester House Years*, North Carolina, 1973.

FORTESCUE, SIR JOHN, *The Correspondence of George III from 1760 to December 1763*, London, 1939. The valuable six volume collection of letters which should, however, be read in conjunction with the volume cited below.

NAMIER, SIR LEWIS B., *Additions and Corrections to Sir John Fortescue's Edition of the Correspondence of George III*, London, 1939.
Personalities and Powers, London, 1955. A collection of essays by the great historian, three of which are devoted to an analysis of George III's role.
The Structure of Politics at the Accession of George III, London, 1957. An outstanding contribution to the debate on the nature of politics in the early years of George III's reign.
England in the Age of the American Revolution, London, 1961. A comprehensive study of the English political background.

BUTTERFIELD, SIR HERBERT, *George III and the Historians*, London, 1957. A sharp and pertinent critique of Namier's approach to political history.

HUNTER, RICHARD, and MACALPINE, IDA, *George III and the Mad Business*, London, 1969. A medico-biographical study of the King. The authors' arguments for porphyria as against insanity have received only limited acceptance by medical opinion.

PARES, RICHARD, *King George III and the Politicians*, London, 1953.

WATSON, STEVEN J., *The Reign of George III*, London, 1960. Like the above title, this provides a wider and more general survey of the period.

II. JOHN WILKES

BLEACKLE, H. W., *The Life of John Wilkes*, London, 1917.

POSTGATE, RAYMOND, *That Devil Wilkes*, London, 1956 (revised edition). The above two volumes provide the fullest biographical accounts.

RUDÉ, GEORGE, *Wilkes and Liberty: A Social Study of 1763 to 1774*, Oxford, 1962.

CHRISTIE, I. R., *Wilkes, Wyvil and Reform: The Parliamentary Reform Movement in British Politics 1760–85*, London, 1962.

III. SAM ADAMS

CUSHING, H. A., *The Writings of Sam Adams*, London, 1904–8. A standard collection of the extant writings.

MILLER, JOHN C., *Sam Adams: Pioneer in Propaganda*, London, 1963. A thorough and detailed biography for the purpose of political history.

BEACH, STEWART, *Samuel Adams: The Fateful Years 1764–76*, London, 1965.

HARLOW, RALPH V., *Samuel Adams, Promoter of the American Revolution*, New York, 1923.

HOSMER, J. K., *Samuel Adams*, London, 1884.

WELLS, WILLIAM V., *The Life and Public Service of Samuel Adams*, London, 1865.

IV. THE AMERICAN REVOLUTION

HOWARD, G. E., *Preliminaries of the Revolution 1763–75*, New York, 1905.

VAN TYNE, C. H., *The American Revolution*, New York, 1905.

TREVELYAN, SIR GEORGE, *The American Revolution*, London, 1899. A major English study, beginning with the Stamp Act and continuing up till 1778.
George III and Charles Fox, London 1912–4. A sympathetic account of American contentions. Especially valuable for its accounts of contemporary English politics.

FISHER, S. G., *The Struggle for American Independence*, London, 1908.

V. GENERAL HISTORIES

GIPSON, L. H., *The Coming of the Revolution*, New York, 1955. An excellent short account of the surge towards independence.

JAMESON, J. F., *The American Revolution Considered as a Social Movement*, Princeton, 1926. The Revolutionary era considered as a period of social and political organisation tending in the direction of democracy. The volume is divided into a series of lectures touching on a wide variety of subjects essential for an understanding of American society.

MILLER, JOHN C., *The Origins of the American Revolution*, Boston, 1943. Places heavy emphasis on the opposed outlooks of the conservative and radical wings of the (American) Whig Party and interprets the Declaration of Independence as a victory for the latter.
Triumph of Freedom, Boston, 1948. A sequel to the above. Though emphasising military history, the author has not neglected the diplomatic, economic, political and idealistic factors that contributed to the American revolution. A chapter is also devoted to the role of propaganda.

MORGAN, E. S., *The Birth of the Republic 1763–89*, Chicago, 1956. A concise presentation of the essential political and constitutional elements in the approach to Independence.

MORGAN, E. S. and H., *The Stamp Act Crisis: Prologue to Revolution*, North Carolina, 1953. Sets forth the general issues which engendered and resulted from the passage of the Stamp Act, whose significance is held to be 'the emergence, not of leaders and methods and organizations, but of well-defined constitutional principles'.

ROBSON, ERIC, *The American Revolution in its Political and Military Aspects 1763–83*, London, 1955. Heightened by the failure of the British Government to understand or adjust to the changing colonial position, a conflict of political ideas, not 'tea and taxes', is argued as the basic cause of the Revolution, with the dominating factor in Britain's defeat being the political isolation produced by the peace settlement of 1763.

VI. HISTORICAL COLLECTIONS

BELOFF, MAX, *The Debate on the American Revolution*, London, 1949. A collection of pamphlets, speeches, etc., in extract with copious notes and annotations. An invaluable sourcebook.

NILES, S. V., *Republication of the Principles and Acts of the American Revolution*, New York, 1876. A revised edition of the 1822 publication compiled by the author's grandfather. A collection of speeches, orations, accounts of men and proceedings plus much neglected material belonging to the Revolutionary period in the USA.